COGNITION AND EMOTION, 2002, *16* (3), 321–330

Cognitive biases in anxiety and depression: Introduction to the Special Issue

Paula T. Hertel

Trinity University, San Antonio, TX, USA

Anxious and depressed people selectively attend to emotionally negative or threatening features of experience. Empirical foundations of that very general truth partly inspired the initiation of the journal *Cognition and Emotion*, and so it is fitting that this Special Issue be dedicated to reports of recent advances in its development. The contributors to the issue hold somewhat different theoretical perspectives on the specific roles of cognitive biases in establishing, maintaining, or reflecting emotional disorders. What they have in common is the belief that selectivity during initial perception or later use of experience is a central cognitive component of anxiety and depression.

These introductory remarks set the stage for the individual contributions by describing a transfer-appropriate-processing framework (Morris, Bransford, & Franks, 1977), adapted to reflect the habits and concerns of people who are anxious, depressed, or both (also see Roediger & McDermott, 1992). Instead of *processing*, I use the terms *attention* and *transfer-appropriate attention* to address a range of cognitive phenomena—including initial perception, subsequent interpretation (attention to specific meanings), and later remembrance (attention to events from the past)—for the purpose of implying that conscious awareness is associated with the phenomena we describe. The framework is merely descriptive, and it borrows heavily from other accounts of disordered cognition (e.g., Williams, Watts, MacLeod, & Mathews, 1997). I intend it to be a heuristic summary of the ways in which anxiety and mood disorders influence and are influenced by mental events. Readers are advised to consult several recent and excellent reviews to obtain fuller accounts of the findings, particu-

Correspondence should be addressed to Paula Hertel, Department of Psychology, Trinity University, 715 Stadium Drive, San Antonio, TX, 78212, USA; e-mail: phertel@trinity.edu

Contributions to this issue describe research presented at a small conference on Clinical Cognition, 18–20 May 2000. The ideas presented in this introduction profit from discussions among the participants: Elaine Fox, Colin MacLeod, Andrew Mathews, Sue Mineka, Susan Nolen-Noeksema, Stephanie Rude, Phil Watkins, and Rich Wenzlaff. The conference was partially funded by Trinity University. I thank Andrew Mathews for comments.

larly concerning our knowledge about specific disorders (e.g., Gotlib, Roberts, & Gilboa, 1996; C. MacLeod, 1999).

ATTENTION AND ITS TRANSFER-APPROPRIATENESS

The term *processing* typically serves as a short-hand expression to represent whatever the individual is mentally doing. *Perceptual processing*, for example, refers to acts of perceiving, and *conceptual processing* to acts that involve meaning. When cognitive acts are performed with awareness of the stimuli in question, they can be thought of as acts of attention. In perceiving a stimulus, we attend to its sensory features, for example. In remembering, we attend to concepts or images from the past (Anderson & Spellman, 1995). These attentional acts are more or less deliberately initiated (or more or less habitually initiated). Moreover, our tendencies to attend to certain features of stimuli more readily than to others are influenced by prior experiences as well as by evolutionarily selected characteristics of the organism (see Oatley & Johnson-Laird, 1987; Öhman & Mineka, 2001). This emphasis on attention benefits discussion of cognition in anxious and depressed people because a selective focus of attention on sources of threat or other matters of personal concern characterises their performance in tasks across the spectrum of perceiving, interpreting, and remembering.

The term *transfer-appropriate attention* implies that current attentional acts, such as interpreting or remembering, can be influenced by similar past attentional acts. Attention is currently guided by habits established during similar past episodes—episodes recruited by elements of the current situation. A fuller description of this episodic approach is given by Neill and Mathis (1998), who described the effects of positive and negative priming in terms of transfer-appropriate and transfer-inappropriate processing. In the latter regard, ignoring an event on one occasion makes it somewhat harder to attend to a similar event later. This analysis extends to transfer across longer time spans and to events no longer present (e.g., the phenomenon of retrieval-induced forgetting, Anderson & Spellman, 1995).

To discuss the range of cognitive biases in terms of selective attention is not meant to deny that sources of bias can occur outside of awareness (see the review by Mogg & Bradley, 1999); instead, the emphasis is placed on the conscious experience of the event receiving that influence. More generally, it seems important not to confuse the degree of attention to the event (e.g., conscious vs. unconscious perception) with the way in which attention comes about (more or less habitually). The contributions to this Special Issue do not address issues regarding unconscious perception, but they do address issues of automaticity with respect to the degree of habit involved in bringing a percept or thought to mind and keeping it there. In that regard, both automatic and controlled cognitive acts participate in instances of biases. Attention can be automatically focused on certain aspects of events, drawn there by habits of perception and conception or by biologically based predispositions. Subsequently, attention is either shifted away from threat (more or less deliberately) or sustained and extended to related experience. The individual is influenced by habit or biology to selectively attend, and then either habit or self control functions to shift or to sustain. Williams et al. (1997) argued that this shift of attention in anxiety—versus the sustaining of attention in depression—is the dimension that differentiates the two general types of disorders.

BIASED ATTENTION IN ANXIETY

People with anxious orientations (as a trait characteristic or as generalised anxiety disorder) are finely tuned to sources of threat in their environment. Some evidence for a similar priority in depression can be found (e.g., McCabe & Gotlib, 1995) but not as consistently; and when it does obtain, anxiety is rarely ruled out. In either case, evidence for vigilance may be restricted to situation in which potentially threatening stimuli compete for attention with less threatening stimuli (see Williams et al., 1997).

In the first contribution to this issue, Mathews and MacLeod remind us about the primary paradigms for demonstrating threat biases in anxiety. In the dot-probe task, for example, anxious participants more quickly identify either the location or the number of dots that occupy the same location immediately vacated by threat (vs. nonthreat) words or faces. In another example, interpretive biases are demonstrated when participants selectively interpret homographs, such as *growth,* in threatening ways. Having themselves collected substantial portions of the evidence regarding anxiety-related biases, some of these investigators' recent efforts have been dedicated to establishing similar biases in nonanxious people, and the current contribution reviews this new body of investigations.

The motivation for Mathews' and MacLeod's efforts to train cognitive biases of course does not emerge from a desire to make people anxious (although they sometimes achieve this end when the task is self-referentially meaningful) or a desire to make people nonanxious (although they hope for eventual clinical application). Instead, their fundamental purpose has been to discover whether cognitive manipulations *can* establish orientations toward threat and subsequent elevation in anxiety. When the manipulation of cognitive biases in a training task transfers to new tasks of perception and interpretation, causal inferences about prior experience become possible, along with causal inferences about the role of cognitive biases in establishing and maintaining anxiety. Mathews and MacLeod also describe a representational model of attention and anxiety that blends an account of these experimental findings with biological considerations. Even from a less representational perspective, however, their research

programmes have produced compelling evidence for the role of transfer-appropriate attention, as it operates apart from any biological tendencies. The outcomes demonstrate that habits to attend selectively can be established in one set of situations and be revealed in other situations that are similarly characterised by options to attend to threatening or nonthreatening aspects.

How we should understand the nature of the selective focus in anxiety is the topic of the next contribution by Fox, Russo, and Dutton. They report three new experiments designed to address the hypothesis of delayed disengagement from threatening events in anxiety. In the normal course of perceiving a novel object, attention is captured and then released. Fox and her colleagues locate the selectivity for threat at the point of release instead of capture and thereby stress the role of prolonged attention or evaluation, in contrast to a pre-attentive mechanism. This distinction was made possible by the use of the cue-validity paradigm, in which anxious participants took longer to respond to probes on trials that had been preceded by threatening cues in the non-predictive location. In subsequent experiments trait-anxious participants (also in anxious states) failed to show the effect of inhibition-of-return to "threatening" locations that they showed to nonthreatening locations. This pattern of findings by Fox and her colleagues is difficult to address from the point of view of a pre-attentive mechanism. Instead, anxiety is believed to be associated with (at least briefly) sustained attention to biologically or socially meaningful events, once they are perceived (a perspective similar to the account by Eysenck, 1982).

Following the early findings of selective attention to threat in anxious states, some researchers questioned whether similar biases might be revealed on indirect tests of memory (see Williams et al., 1997). Because selectivity occurs in automatic ways on tasks like the dot-probe procedure, they reasoned, it should also be revealed on tests that reflect automatic or nondeliberate uses of memory. Prior experience in selecting particular items should bolster their selection on the current indirect test. Yet, studies examining implicit memory biases in anxiety have shown inconsistent results, perhaps partly because a close match between study and test has not been achieved (see C. MacLeod, 1999). According to a transfer-appropriate approach, any advantage conferred by prior experience should result from the similarity between the procedures of selection on the two occasions. To date, however, evidence for implicit biases has been clearest under conditions that seem transfer *inappropriate*, such as when letter fragments are used to cue the production of words that were previously processed conceptually (Williams et al., 1997). Although it has been difficult to gain experimental control of attention in implicit-memory experiments without "giving away" the nature of the test, matching the options for attention across study and test might be a profitable goal for future research. Similar issues and challenges also pertain to the domain of depression-related biases in implicit memory.

BIASED ATTENTION IN DEPRESSION

Most evidence for depression-related bias is found on tests of explicit memory. Depressed participants tend to recall negatively valenced words more frequently than do nondepressed participants and more frequently than they themselves recall positively valenced words. Sometimes the interaction of group and type of material takes the form of the absence of a positive bias in the depressed group instead of the presence of a negative bias. Regardless, the relationship between emotional state and the nature of the events recalled is beyond dispute in depressed samples, and when it does occur in anxious samples those participants tend to be depressed as well (see Williams et al., 1997). In the language of a transfer-appropriate framework, depressed people selectively attend to negatively toned past events during their attempts to remember—events that presumably have incurred previous preferential attention and consideration. This prediction easily encompasses instances of biased autobiographical recall as well as performance in laboratory tasks. Of course, only in laboratory studies do we have access to the nature of attention during the initial event that is later remembered, for the purpose of addressing the issue of transfer appropriateness.

What do we know about the selectivity of attention during initial exposure, the so-called encoding phase of memory experiments? Unfortunately, we have little evidence of the degree to which attention is sustained differentially according to emotional valence (cf. Wenzlaff, Meier, & Salas, this issue). Instead, investigators have tended to vary the type of task performed, while holding constant features such as exposure duration. Depression-congruent recall typically is found only for materials that appear in conceptual encoding tasks, and so it is assumed that negative materials have been better elaborated during the time allotted, perhaps by relation to other negative thoughts. This assumption is bolstered by evidence of differential activation in frontal regions of the brain, according to mood state and emotional valence of materials (see Davidson, 1999). Of course, tendencies toward differential elaboration might develop in part from habits of thinking about (remembering) negative events in one's life. Indeed, self-referential tasks seem to be required in order to obtain evidence for mood-congruent recall in clinical depression (see Gotlib et al., 1996). Self-referential thoughts are readily available to serve as guides to attention later on, when recall is requested, and depression-congruent memories are thereby produced. In short, elaboration and recall seem to involve very similar acts of biased attention.

If depression-related memory biases can be understood in terms of transfer-appropriate attention, they should also be revealed by performance on indirect tests, when the tasks and their contexts invite the same or similar selectivity. When the task used for the indirect test of memory allows variation in the nature of what comes to mind, performance should show the effects of prior differential attention and thought. Sometimes it does. Watkins' contribution to this issue summarises the research that he and his colleagues have conducted from a transfer-appropriate perspective, including manipulations of the focus of attention during the initial task and nature of the procedures used on the indirect test. Not surprisingly, determining how to match the cognitive acts on both occasions in ways that facilitate transfer of selectivity turns out to be not an easy task. Many of the challenges encountered in process-oriented research pertain to the fact that tasks invite multiple procedures and concomitant shifts in transfer potential. Nevertheless, Watkins' research suggests that conceptual tasks for testing are required for showing implicit-memory biases in depression (as is true for explicit-memory biases). It's the *thought* that counts, when it comes to revealing biased use of prior experience. But as Watkins also argues, the use of a conceptually oriented test is not sufficient to produce the effect. According to the present framework, a clear opportunity for selection among alternative responses during the indirect test might also be important, much like what happens on direct tests of memory. Explicit biases are revealed most clearly on tests of free recall—tests with the fewest constraints on attention. The indirect test of free association seems to be less constrained than other conceptual indirect tests, but perhaps too much so, in the sense that "nonconceptual" associations might be invoked (see Watkins' discussion of inconsistent findings with this test). In general, the opportunity to select among concepts that differ in emotional meaning should play an important role in revealing biases.

Watkins's concluding remarks remind us that reasoning about biases in memory relies fundamentally on both clinical and laboratory evidence of rumination in depression. Rumination stands as the classic case of sustained biased attention to certain features of past (and possible future) experience. The connection between rumination and memory has been addressed explicitly by Teasdale and Nolen-Hoeksema (see Nolen-Hoeksema, 2000; Teasdale & Barnard, 1993). In ruminative episodes, the depressed person continues to think repetitively about negatively toned events and their interpretations. The often intense focus of attention during rumination suggests that it involves a high degree of cognitive control, but not in the sense that ruminative episodes need be initiated deliberately, nor in the sense that they can be interrupted or curtailed at will (see Hertel, 2000). Negative thoughts spring into mind automatically and subsequently invite other related thoughts, and a *lack of* wilful control is shown by difficulties in switching attention to other matters. An example of the latter can be seen in an experiment that used procedures developed by Nolen-Hoeksema to invite ruminative or distracting thoughts during a retention interval prior to a memory test for emotionally neutral materials (Hertel, 1998). In the group of dysphoric students, compared to the controls, controlled recollection was impaired following ruminative but not distracting thoughts. In this way, rumination is transfer-*inappropriate* for all but future episodes of rumination or other similar tasks (such as the recall of negative materials). Once begun, it is difficult to halt.

Although rumination is not directly addressed, the final two contributions to this issue emphasise the relation of current thoughts, interpretations, and memory biases to past or future depression. From a clinical perspective, these studies provide evidence regarding vulnerability to depression in the form of biased performance on cognitive tasks. During the first phase in the study by Wenzlaff, Meier, and Salas, participants rated the emotional value of positive, negative, and emotionally ambiguous statements and indicated the degree of uncertainty about each rating. Degree of uncertainty about their ratings for ambiguous statements was positively correlated with later false recognition of negative disambiguations; if they felt uncertain they later tended to remember the ambiguous statements as negative. This was true both for dysphoric participants and for the participants who had been dysphoric earlier in the semester but were no longer feeling that way (but not for those who were nondysphoric throughout the semester). Wenzlaff et al. were especially interested in the relationship shown by previously dysphoric participants who seemed to be likely candidates for using thought suppression. Their performance implied that prior real-world experience with depressive interpretations can override current motivations to avoid negative thoughts and transfer to new ambiguous situations.

The final contribution to this issue, by Rude, Wenzlaff, Gibbs, Vane, and Whitney, addresses the other side of the coin: Do habits of attending to negative meanings predict future depressive symptoms? Their investigation is among the first to find evidence for this prospective prediction (also see Alloy, Abramson, & Francis, 1999; Nolen-Hoeksema, 2000). Habits in negative thinking were revealed in a task that required selection of interpretations for word strings. When participants showed negatively biased interpretations under conditions that hampered mental control, they were subsequently more likely to experience depressive symptoms a few weeks later. This result obtained, regardless of participants' prior experience with depression, and it bolsters our confidence in the contributory role of attentional biases in the development of emotional disorders. The participants who would later become dysphoric selectively attended to the more negative of the alternative conceptual structures that were available to them, not unlike the participants in studies described by Mathews and MacLeod who temporarily experienced increased anxiety after they were trained to notice and interpret threat.

SIMILARITIES AND DIFFERENCES

The search for distinguishing cognitive features of emotional disorders has been complicated by the high rate of comorbidity of anxious and depressive features. Mineka, Watson, and Clark's (1998) approach to understanding such cooccurrence identifies possible common and unique components to the syndromes of anxiety and depression. The common component seems to be general distress, with the differentiating components developing from that more general base (see Widiger & Clark, 2000).

A componential approach easily accommodates evidence for cognitive biases. The common cognitive feature appears to be the tendency to attend initially to threat and negativity and to show that selectivity in dwell times or semantic interpretations. Anxious people dwell (if only briefly) on threatening stimuli and perceive threat in ambiguous events. Although we do not yet know if depressed or dysphoric people show delayed dwell times (see Fox et al., this issue), their ruminative styles certainly qualify as prolonged attention to negative thoughts, and they do evidence negative selectivity in initial interpretations. When thought control is hampered, habits to see the world in negative ways predict depressive symptomology later on (Rude et al., this issue). Similarly, deliberately trained habits of interpretation can give rise to anxious states (Mathews & MacLeod, this issue), and ruminative tendencies predict future symptoms of anxiety as well as symptoms of depression (Nolen-Hoeksema, 2000). Depression and anxiety have a lot in common cognitively.

Building on ideas proposed by Williams et al. (1997) and others, a successful pursuit of differences might be one that examines the length and quality of the "dwell times", predicated on the specific goals of avoidance (in anxiety) or resolution (in depression). The paucity of evidence regarding elaborative biases in anxiety leads us to think that anxiety is closely associated with turning attention away from sources of threat at some point beyond the initial capture, probably in order to avoid increases in anxiety. Yet, there is some evidence for similar patterns of avoidance in depressed states. For example, formerly dysphoric people suppress negative thoughts (Wenzlaff et al., this issue), perhaps because they have learned to dread habitual rumination. And temporarily sad people sometimes show evidence of mood-*incongruent* memory if they are high in self control (see Parrott, 1994), which suggests that they avoid negative thoughts initially or at the time of the memory test. Therefore, the length or quality of dwelling does not distinguish between anxiety and depression in a very straightforward way.

Another possible basis for distinguishing between cognitive patterns in anxiety and those in depression is to consider whether attention is focused mainly on past or future events. Ruminative acts, almost by definition, typically focus on past events, and this clinical pattern corresponds to depression-related biases during memory tests. In contrast, one identifying feature of anxiety is worry, which is clearly future oriented (see Eysenck, 1982). Prospective judgements tend to be more negatively toned in anxious states, compared to depressed states (which are associated with an absence of positivity; see the review by A. MacLeod, 1999). Whether the habitual cognitions of the individual are past or future oriented should be taken into account because such habits likely develop during unstructured intervals and transfer to similarly unstructured laboratory and real-world tasks.

In summary, the findings described in this Special Issue come together to emphasise similarities between anxious and depressed cognition, in the form of habitual attention to negativity or threat. Moreover, several contributions help us to consider these habits as causes and not just concomitants and consequences of emotional disorder. An important question in the realm of both disorders therefore concerns subsequent control of attention, beyond the initial focus. The contributions to this issue bring to mind the possibility of training not just habits of initial attention, but habits of intentional control (see Jacoby, Jennings, & Hay; 1996). As a result of these and similar experimental efforts, therapeutic techniques based on transfer-appropriate training have available a growing body of evidence to justify and guide their development.

REFERENCES

Alloy, L.B., Abramson, L.Y., & Francis, E.L. (1999). Do negative cognitive styles confer vulnerability to depression? *Current Directions in Psychological Science, 8,* 128–132.

Anderson, M.C., & Spellman, B.A. (1995). On the status of inhibitory mechanisms in cognition: Memory retrieval as a model case. *Psychological Review, 102,* 68–100.

Davidson, R.J. (1999). Neuropsychological perspectives on affective styles and their cognitive consequences. In T. Dalgleish & M. Power (Eds.), *Handbook of cognition and emotion* (pp.103–124). Chichester, UK: Wiley.

Eysenck, M. (1982). *Attention and arousal: Cognition and performance.* Berlin: Springer.

Gotlib, I.H., Roberts, J.E., & Gilboa, E. (1996). Cognitive interference in depression. In I.G. Sarason, G.R. Pierce, & B.R. Sarason, (Eds.), *Cognitive interference: Theories, methods, and findings* (pp. 347–377). Mahwah, NJ: Erlbaum.

Hertel, P.T. (1998). The relationship between rumination and impaired memory in dysphoric moods. *Journal of Abnormal Psychology, 107,* 166–172.

Hertel, P.T. (2000). The cognitive-initiative account of depression-related impairments in memory. In D. Medin (Ed.), *The psychology of learning and motivation* (Vol. 39, pp. 47–71). New York: Academic Press.

Jacoby, L.L., Jennings, J.M., & Hay, J.F. (1996). Dissociating automatic and consciously controlled processes: Implications for diagnosis and rehabilitation of memory deficits. In D. Herrmann, C. McEvoy, C. Herzog, P.T. Hertel, & M.K. Johnson (Eds.), *Basic and applied memory research: Theory in context* (pp. 161–194). Mahwah, NJ: Erlbaum.

MacLeod, A.K. (1999). Prospective cognitions. In T. Dalgleish & M. Power (Eds.), *Handbook of cogniton and emotion* (pp.267–280). Chichester, UK: Wiley.

MacLeod, C. (1999). Anxiety and anxiety disorders. In T. Dalgleish & M. Power (Eds.), *Handbook of cogniton and emotion* (pp.447–478). Chichester, UK: Wiley.

McCabe, S.B., & Gotlib, Ian H. (1995). Selective attention and clinical depression: Performance on a deployment-of-attention task. *Journal of Abnormal Psychology, 104,* 241–245.

Mineka, S., Watson, D., & Clark, L.A. (1998). Comorbidity of anxiety and unipolar mood disorders. *Annual Review of Psychology, 49,* 377–412.

Mogg, K., & Bradley, B.P. (1999). Selective attention and anxiety: A cognitive-motivational perspective. In T. Dalgleish & M. Power (Eds.), *Handbook of cogniton and emotion* (pp.145–170). Chichester, UK: Wiley.

Morris, C.D., Bransford, J.D., & Franks, J.J. (1977). Levels of processing versus transfer-appropriate processing. *Journal of Verbal Learning and Verbal Behavior, 16,* 519–533.

Neill, W.T., & Mathis, K.M. (1998). Transfer-inappropriate processing: Negative priming and related phenomena. In D. Medin (Ed.), *The psychology of learning and motivation* (Vol. 38, pp. 1–44). New York: Academic Press.

Nolen-Hoeksema, S. (2000). The role of rumination in depressive disorders and mixed anxiety/depressive symptoms. *Journal of Abnormal Psychology, 109,* 504–511.

Oatley, K., & Johnson-Laird, P. (1987). Toward a cognitive theory of emotions. *Cognition and Emotion, 1,* 29–50.

Öhman, A., & Mineka, S. (2001). Fears, phobias, and preparedness: Toward an evolved module of fear and fear learning. *Psychological Review, 108,* 483–522.

Parrott, W.G., (1994). An association between emotional self-control and mood-incongruent recall. In N. H. Frijda (Ed.), *Proceedings of the VIIIth Conference of the International Society for Research on Emotions* (pp. 313–317). Storrs, CT: International Society for Research on Emotions.

Roediger, H.L., & McDermott, K.B. (1992). Depression and implicit memory: A commentary. *Journal of Abnormal Psychology, 101,* 587–591.

Teasdale, J.D., & Barnard, P.J. (1993). *Affect, cognition, and change: Re-modeling depressive thought.* Hove, UK: Lawrence Erlbaum Associates Ltd.

Widiger, T.A, & Clark, L.A. (2000). Toward *DSM-V* and the classification of psychopathology. *Psychological Bulletin, 126,* 946–963.

Williams, J.M.G., Watts, F.N., MacLeod, C., Mathews, A. (1997). *Cognitive psychology and emotional disorders* (2nd ed.). Chichester, UK: Wiley.

COGNITION AND EMOTION, 2002, 16 (3), 331–354

Induced processing biases have causal effects on anxiety

Andrew Mathews

MRC Cognition and Brain Sciences Unit, Cambridge, UK

Colin MacLeod

University of Western Australia, Nedlands, Australia

After briefly describing the nature of emotional processing biases associated with vulnerability to anxiety, and a model of how they may be produced, we review new data on the experimental induction of attentional and interpretative biases. We show that these biases can be readily induced in the laboratory, in the absence of mood changes. However, induced biases exert effects on the processing of new information and cause congruent changes in state anxiety when they influence how emotionally significant information is encoded. We can therefore conclude that biases have causal effects on vulnerability to anxiety via their influence on how significant events are processed. Finally, we discuss how our model might account for the acquisition of processing bias and for when they can influence anxiety.

The nature of anxiety-linked processing biases

In everyday life we commonly encounter events that have both negative and positive aspects, or are ambiguous in their emotional meaning. Which aspect we attend to, or how we interpret such ambiguity, is associated with enduring tendencies to experience positive or negative emotional states, such as anxiety, as well as current mood (for a review, see Mathews & MacLeod, 1994). Thus, when two or more stimuli or meanings compete for processing resources, people with high levels of trait anxiety—particularly when under stress—are more likely than are others to attend to a negatively valenced or threatening stimulus,

Correspondence should be addressed to Andrew Mathews, MRC Cognition and Brain Sciences Unit 15, Chaucer Road, Cambridge, CB2 2EF, UK; e-mail: andrew.mathews@mrc-cbu.ac.uk, or Colin MacLeod, Department of Psychology, University of Western Australia, Nedlands, WA 6907, Australia; e-mail: colin@psych.uwa.edu.au

Several of the experiments reported here were carried out by Lynlee Campbell as part of her doctoral research work. We thank Bundy Mackintosh and Tom Borkovec for helpful theoretical discussions.

http://www.tandf.co.uk/journals/pp/02699931.html   DOI:10.1080/02699930143000518

and are more likely to adopt a threatening interpretation of ambiguous information.

For example, if two words differing in their valence are displayed simultaneously and are followed by a to-be-detected target, high trait-anxious individuals under stress are typically faster to detect targets in the prior location of a threatening word. In low trait anxious individuals this effect is typically absent, or sometimes reversed, even under stressful conditions (e.g., MacLeod & Mathews, 1988). Of course, it would not be adaptive for anyone, regardless of trait anxiety, to ignore *all* threatening information, because many events require attention and positive action to avert real danger. Indeed, it seems self-evident that our survival depends on responding to major threats to personal safety. The distinction between those with high versus low trait anxiety thus refers to their responsiveness to more minor threat cues that do not signal dangers requiring urgent action.

There are a number of ways in which one could try to account for this difference in responsiveness. One possibility is that there is some kind of threat evaluation process, with a threshold that must be exceeded before the cognitive system shifts from a mode in which threat cues can be ignored, to one in which they are attended. If so, then it could be the threshold level at which this shift occurs that is associated with vulnerability to anxiety. As indicated earlier, there is evidence showing that attention to minor threat cues (vigilance) is revealed by stress in high, but not in low trait anxious individuals (MacLeod & Mathews, 1988).

Differences between high and low trait-anxious individuals are not confined to experiments involving words. Equivalent results have been found using displays of two faces varying in emotional expression (Mogg & Bradley, 1999; but see Mansell, Clark, Ehlers & Chen, 1999 for discrepant results in social anxiety) or with other pictures varying in their threatening content (Yiend & Mathews, 2001). This last study reported experiments in which single pictures varying in emotional valence were presented in one location, followed by a target in the same or in another location. This method allows a distinction to be drawn between the speeding due to attentional engagement with a picture if the target appears in the same location, and slowing when participants must disengage attention to find a target elsewhere. Evidence from this last study, and from other similar research (e.g., Compton, 2000; Fox, Russo, Bowles & Dutton, 2001) strongly suggests that these effects arise because anxiety-prone individuals have greater difficulty in *disengaging* attentional resources from threatening information.

Related interference effects occur when threatening stimuli must be ignored in order to perform a task efficiently. For example, in highly anxious individuals, search for a neutral target is slowed if it is embedded among threatening distracters (Mathews, May, Mogg & Eysenck, 1990). Anxious individuals also show greater interference when colour-naming threatening words (the emotional

Stroop effect, see Williams, Mathews, & MacLeod, 1996). This effect persists even when the words are displayed very briefly and are followed by an obscuring mask to restrict awareness (e.g., MacLeod & Rutherford, 1992; Mogg, Bradley, Williams, & Mathews, 1993). Stroop interference from masked words has also been found in one study to predict later distress following a disturbing life event (MacLeod & Hagan, 1992). Both faster detection of targets replacing threatening words, and related interference effects, may thus arise from the same basic process, initiated outside awareness, in which mildly threatening stimuli capture attentional resources more readily in high trait anxious individuals.

When reading about events that are ambiguous in terms of their emotional implications, individuals having low scores on measures of trait anxiety are more likely to arrive at positive interpretations, whereas those with high scores appear to be more even-handed or to favour more threatening interpretations. Thus, after hearing the sentence *"The doctor examined little Emma's growth"*, nonanxious controls were more likely than anxious patients to endorse related recognition items referring to height as opposed to cancer (Eysenck, Mogg, May, Richards, & Mathews, 1991). When reading more complex and realistic descriptions of social situations, speeded lexical decisions for words matching valenced inferences at points of ambiguity show similar effects (e.g., Hirsch & Mathews, 1997, 2000). These differences may reflect selective processes related to those discussed above. Threatening meanings of ambiguous events may be more likely to capture attentional resources in anxiety-prone individuals, and thus be preferentially encoded.

The relationship between processing biases and vulnerability to anxiety

The fact that these processing biases are associated with individual differences in trait anxiety has led many researchers—including ourselves—to speculate about the causal relationship between bias and vulnerability to anxiety. We have previously suggested that vulnerability to anxiety is associated with different processing styles that are elicited by stressful events (e.g., Williams, Watts, MacLeod, & Mathews, 1997; see also Mogg & Bradley, 1998). In vulnerable individuals, a stressful event, such as an upcoming examination or a medical diagnosis, is more likely to elicit a "vigilant" processing mode, in which attention is readily captured by relatively mild threatening cues. Consequently, these individuals will in effect be exposed to a stream of information about possible dangers, leading to increased anxiety. In less vulnerable people, however, the same event may be insufficient to trigger a shift from the default "avoidant" mode, in which threatening information is ignored. According to this hypothesis, it is the type of processing style, or bias, that is elicited by events which causes vulnerability to anxiety, instead of biased processing being only an incidental by-product of emotional variations.

The critical characteristic of those prone to excessive anxiety, on this view, is that the level of threat sufficient to cause switching from avoidance to a vigilant processing mode is too low. Consequently, these vulnerable individuals respond vigilantly in a rather all-or-none manner, being unable to disengage attention from any threat-related cues or meanings, no matter how mild or irrelevant to current goals they may be. A previous attempt to model a system that could account for these effects (Mathews & Mackintosh, 1998; Mathews, Mackintosh & Fulcher, 1997) is briefly described below.

MODELLING ANXIETY-LINKED PROCESSING BIASES

Attentional and interpretative biases can be observed only when at least two competing processing options are present, which differ in their emotional valence. No associations with individual differences in anxiety proneness have been found in tasks when one emotional or neutral stimulus is presented as a single target (e.g., Mathews & Milroy, 1994). However, such associations do emerge when two or more possible targets are present simultaneously (MacLeod & Mathews, 1991; Mogg, Mathews, Eysenck, & May, 1991; see also Byrne & Eysenck, 1995). Mathews and Mackintosh (1998) took these findings to support the hypothesis that internal representations corresponding to the two (or more) processing options compete for attention (modelled as activation level) via inhibitory links. As one representation gains activation it inhibits the other, until the dominant representation succeeds in capturing attention and access to awareness. Normally, controlled task demand increases the activation of the intended target, which then inhibits attention to an irrelevant distracter. However, if a distracter matches information associated with threat, it may receive additional activation from a postulated threat evaluation system, and so will compete more effectively for attention (see Figure 1).

Output from this nonconscious evaluation system is supposed to selectively activate perceptual representations which have been biologically prepared in the course of evolution, or have well learned associations with danger and require only the matching of perceptual input to previously computed evaluations. Thus a perceptual cue previously linked with aversive stimuli or experiences could acquire the capacity to activate fear responses without further higher level processing.

Evidence supporting the existence of such a threat evaluation system includes animal research showing that well learned fear cues can elicit fear responses via a ''short-cut'' route from the thalamus direct to the amygdala (LeDoux, 1995). In humans, threatening pictures elicit more neural activity in primary visual cortex than do neutral scenes, perhaps due to re-entrant projections from the amygdala (Lang et al., 1998). Pictures of snakes elicit skin conductance responses in snake-fearful individuals, even when the pictures are masked to prevent conscious identification (Öhman & Soares, 1994, 1998). Although it could be argued that pictures activate biologically prepared representations, this cannot be the case with masked words, which can have similar effects (Van den Hout, de Jong, & Kindt, 2000). Thus, threatening pictures or arbitrary learned symbols such as valenced words—even when masked to prevent awareness— can activate orienting responses and disrupt attention to an ongoing task in anxious individuals (see also MacLeod & Rutherford, 1992; Mogg et al., 1993).

There are reciprocal connections between areas in the frontal cortex and the amygdala, suggesting that both may be involved in the control of different aspects of the response to anxiety-evoking events (Kalin, Shelton, Davidson, & Kelley, 2001; Rolls, 1999). Brain imaging research in humans has suggested reciprocal inhibition between attention to neutral targets and to emotional distracters, within the anterior cingulate (Bush, Luu, & Posner, 2000; Drevets & Raichle, 1998). In several experiments, threatening words in the emotional Stroop task have been found to activate the "affective" division of the cingulate, but the same area is deactivated when subjects attend to emotionally neutral information within a similar task. Hence, the function of the cingulate may be to monitor for processing conflicts and when they are detected, to recruit other frontal areas to inhibit the interfering distracter (MacDonald, Cohen, Stenger, &

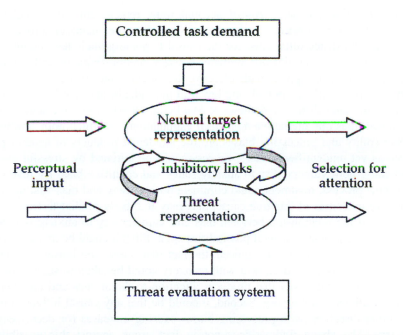

Figure 1. Schematic outline of the model proposed by Mathews and Mackintosh (1998). Representations of neutral targets, activated by task demand processes, compete for attention via mutual inhibitory links with emotional distractors activated by a nonconscious threat evaluation system.

Carter, 2000). Interference from, and attention to, an emotional distracter thus depends on whether the activation accruing from automatic affective processing exceeds the competing controlled activation of an intended target.

To summarise the model, we suppose that variations in vulnerability to anxiety under stress are the joint product of two interacting processes that determine the extent to which threatening cues or meanings succeed in holding attention. The first of these is due to the operation of a system that evaluates threat and provides activation to the corresponding internal representations. The second depends on an executive attentional system that determines the degree to which this activation can be opposed by controlled effort. Even if threat cues are detected, they may be inhibited and thus not encoded, at the cost of making more task-related effort. However, under certain conditions, such as when stress or mental load is high, the capacity limits on maintaining this effort may be exceeded and control will fail. If this occurs, then the stream of information entering awareness will become dominated by threat-related information (the "vigilant processing mode"), and state anxiety will increase as a result.

TESTING THE CAUSAL STATUS OF PROCESSING BIASES

It is clear that any such *causal* account must remain entirely speculative, however, if for no other reason than that all the relevant evidence is correlational in nature. Evidence often cited for the causal hypothesis includes findings that emotional processing bias differentiates between anxious patients and controls, that differences disappear with effective treatment, that stressful events can induce differential bias in high and low trait individuals, and that bias measures can predict later distress (Mathews & MacLeod, 1994). However, none of this evidence rules out alternative *noncausal* explanations, in which both emotional vulnerability and processing biases are the incidental products of another process, as yet unidentified. Such a process could be initiated by stressful events and cause both vulnerability to anxiety states and cognitive bias. By reversing the same process, treatment could eliminate both anxiety and bias, and because both are outcomes of this true cause, bias may indirectly predict distress.

Even if the relationship between bias and vulnerability to anxiety is indeed causal, this still leaves several possibilities open. First, it could be that anxiety is a cause of processing biases. Indeed, the fact that processing biases associated with anxiety disorders disappear with recovery could be taken to suggest that it is the anxiety state itself that produces attention to threat cues and threatening interpretations of ambiguity. Second, it could be that any causal influence is in the other direction, with processing biases causing increases (or decreases) in anxiety. The above finding does not in fact argue against this possibility, because recovery could begin with a shift out of the "vigilant processing mode" which then causes anxiety reduction. Third, both directions of causality may operate together in some kind of interactive process. Our own view is closest to this third possibility. We have suggested that high trait anxiety is associated with a lower threshold for shifting into a vigilant processing mode. Thus we suppose that stressful events induce a vigilant mode more readily in some individuals, and the preferential encoding of threat cues that results then serves to increase or maintain the tendency to experience anxious mood states.

In the present paper we focus on the hypothesis that induced processing biases can cause anxiety, while leaving open the possibility that causal effects could also operate in the reverse direction, providing a feedback loop. As already indicated, the observed correlations between processing bias and anxiety do not rule out noncausal alternatives. The only decisive method of testing the hypothesis that bias can cause anxiety is thus to manipulate processing bias directly.

We review here the results of experiments designed to do precisely this, and demonstrate that vulnerability to experience anxiety can indeed be altered by such experimental manipulations. Importantly, however, we show that it is not the procedures employed to induce bias that alter anxiety directly. Rather, it is only when the induced bias is actively deployed to process personally significant events that changes occur. Put another way, the potential for biased processing can be induced by appropriate training procedures, without observable changes in anxiety. However, when later faced with a significant emotional event that could be processed in different ways, depending on the direction of bias that was induced, congruent changes in anxiety then emerge.

PROCEDURES FOR EXPERIMENTALLY INDUCING ATTENTIONAL BIAS

In a series of experiments carried out by MacLeod and colleagues, notably Lynlee Campbell and Elizabeth Rutherford at the University of Western Australia, several different methods have been used to induce attentional bias in volunteers.[1] Initially, participants were students with trait anxiety scores in the middle range, so that pre-existing emotional biases were unlikely to be marked. In general, the method used was to assign students at random to one of two training conditions. One condition was intended to induce attention to threatening cues and the other to induce avoidance of such threatening cues in favour of emotionally neutral stimuli. The first four experiments described here were designed to develop and pilot possible training tasks that could be used to induce

---

[1] Experiments numbered here as 1–8 are unpublished at the time of writing. Some form part of a PhD thesis submitted to the University of Western Australia by Lynlee Campbell. Experiments 5 and 6 form part of a paper in press with the *Journal of Abnormal Psychology* (MacLeod, Rutherford, Campbell, Ebsworthy, & Holker, 2001).

attentional effects. In later experiments (experiments 5–8 in this review), the effects of a trained bias on anxiety induced by a stressful event was also assessed.

In the first pilot experiment, a series of words with either threatening or neutral meanings (e.g., cancer, ceiling) were displayed one at a time on a computer screen, and participants were required either to make a grammar judgement or to name the colour in which the word was displayed. For example, if the word "death" was displayed in red, followed by the cue "colour?" the participant was required to respond "red". If the word "window" was displayed in green followed by the cue "noun?" the participant was required to respond "yes". The underlying assumption was that efficient colour naming is possible—and indeed may be facilitated—if word meanings are ignored. However, word meaning must be at least minimally attended in order to make judgements about grammar.

The critical manipulation was that in one group ($n = 13$) participants were consistently given instructions to make grammar judgements (and thus access word meaning) following words with threatening meanings, and to name colours after neutral words (not requiring access to meaning). The other group ($n = 14$) was given the converse instructions: To name the colour of threatening words and to make grammar judgements for neutral words. After 384 of these "training" trials, both groups went on to 192 test trials in which the response instructions for each valence of word were randomly varied. Analyses of response latencies in these test trials revealed significant interactions between training group and word valence for both the colour naming ($p < .01$) and grammatical decision tasks ($p < .001$). Latencies to colour name words for which that participant had previously made a grammatical judgement were significantly slower than for previously colour named words, and vice versa for grammar judgements.

Of course, these results can be readily explained by noting that it is easier to repeat a decision made previously for a particular stimulus, than to make another equally well practised decision that has not previously been applied to that stimulus. Thus, although the grammatical decisions used here were intended to force access to word meanings, there is no compelling reason to believe that the training effect depended on selective encoding due to word valence. This issue will come up in later experiments, where it will be shown that training effects extend to words that were never exposed during training, but were related in valence to those that had been. At this stage we will note only that those participants trained to make grammatical decisions for threatening words were slower, by approximately 40 ms, to name the colour of threatening words during test trials than were those who had practised naming their colour. This magnitude of slowing in colour-naming latencies for threatening words is similar to the mean of emotional Stroop interference effects seen in clinically anxious groups (see Williams et al., 1996).

In three further pilot experiments variable results were obtained using different methods. In Experiment 2, angry or happy faces were presented in monochrome colour-tinted displays and subjects were required to make either age judgements or to report the colour in which the face was displayed. One group consistently colour-named angry faces and made age judgements for happy faces, while the other group did the reverse. Although on test trials the apparent difference in mean latencies was similar to the previous experiment, it did not reach statistical significance.

Experiment 3 was modelled on our earlier finding, replicated in several subsequent studies, that anxious patients detected targets in the prior location of threatening words faster than those in the prior location of neutral words, unlike controls (MacLeod, Mathews, & Tata, 1986). In the present adaptation of this task, two words, one with a threatening meaning and one with a neutral meaning, were displayed for 500 ms, followed by a target to be identified (one or two dots) appearing in the prior location of one or other of these words. Participants had to press one of two keys, corresponding to target identity, as quickly as they could. Over 576 training trials, these targets always appeared in the location of threatening words, or in that of neutral words, depending on random group assignment ($n = 16$ in each group).

In 128 test trials that were interleaved over the second half of training, targets appeared in either location with equal frequency. Analysis of latencies in these test trials revealed a significant interaction of group with type of word probed ($p < .01$). Participants trained to attend to threat word locations were generally slower (by about 25 ms), to detect targets appearing in the location of neutral words in test trials than were participants in the other group. The direction of this difference between groups was reversed when test trial targets appeared in the location of threatening words.

Experiment 4 used the same task, with the difference that pairs of faces, depicting the same person with angry and happy expressions, replaced the words used previously. Analysis of latencies derived from test trials interleaved as before again revealed a significant interaction between group and type of facial expression probed, $p < .01$. When a target appeared in the location of a happy face, the group trained to attend to angry faces had slower latencies than did the other group, and vice versa when a target appeared in the location of angry faces. Thus, summarising across these pilot experiments, reliable training effects were achieved when targets to be detected consistently appeared in the location of words or faces of the designated valence. We turn now to experiments that used the methods developed in these pilot studies to directly address the question of whether training effects generalise to novel exemplars, and whether they influence the response to stress.

EFFECTS OF INDUCED ATTENTIONAL BIAS ON EMOTIONAL VULNERABILITY

In experiments 5 and 6 (reported in MacLeod et al., 2001) the training method used the same number of threat/neutral word pair trials as in experiment 3, but with larger numbers of participants ($n = 32$ in each group). As before, for one group (attend threat), a target (one or two dots) always replaced the threatening word after 500 ms during training trials, with participants required to identify the target by pressing one of two keys as fast as possible. For the other group (avoid threat) targets always replaced neutral words.

In addition, however, several new features were introduced. First, the 96 test trials distributed through training, in which the target locations were not contingent on word position, were divided into half that used old word pairs and half that employed words never previously exposed in training. Each set was further divided into those presented for approximately 500 ms, allowing easy identification of words, and those presented for only 20 ms before being replaced by an obscuring mask to reduce awareness. Second, at the end of the experiment, both groups were exposed to a mildly stressful experience, consisting of attempting to solve 30 either difficult or insoluble anagrams under timed conditions while being videotaped. Negative mood was assessed before and after this task using two visual analogue scales (range 1–30), one for rating anxiety and one for depressed mood.

In an analysis of test trial latencies, there was a significant interaction of group by exposure duration by valence of word probed, $p < .05$. There were no significant effects for the 20 ms exposure trials, but the group by word valence interaction remained significant for 500 ms exposure trials. Both groups were faster when the "expected" word locations were probed. More importantly, when only new word trials were analysed, the same interaction remained significant, $p < .05$. That is, those trained to attend threat were faster to detect targets in the location of new threatening words (by about 30 ms), than were those in the other ("avoid threat") group. This difference attributable to training was reversed in the case of targets replacing new neutral words. Importantly, therefore, training seems to induce a general set to attend to all threatening words (or otherwise), rather than just those words that have been exposed previously during training. However, this effect did not appear to survive masking in which the critical words were exposed under conditions of restricted awareness.

Immediately after training, but before the stress task, mood scores were essentially identical across training groups. Negative mood assessed immediately after the post-training stress task showed increases on both scales for both groups, but these were marginally greater in those trained to attend threatening words rather than to avoid them (group × time interaction, $p < .06$, not further qualified by type of scale).

Given this important but marginally reliable effect, the above procedure was replicated in experiment 6, but with an increased number of training trials (768). Test trials (96) were given before as well as immediately after training, and consisted only of new words, never used in training, presented for 500 ms. The stress task was also given twice, before and after training and both anxious and depressed mood was assessed pre- and post-stress on each occasion.

Before training, group differences in test trial latencies did not approach significance. After training, the group by target location interaction revealed a nonsignificant trend, $p < .07$, reflecting the tendency for those trained to attend threat to be slightly faster than the other group (by 14 ms) to identify targets in the location of new threatening words. Both groups showed equivalent increases in negative mood due to the stress task prior to training, but this effect did not differ across groups. After training, however, there was a significant interaction of group by time, $p < .05$, not further qualified by type of mood scale. Mean ratings for both groups were nearly identical prior to the stress task, and did not change in the "avoid threat" group, but increased significantly ($p < .01$) in the group trained to attend to threat.

An index of attention to threat in each set of test trials was computed by subtracting the latencies to detect targets in the locations of threat from those in the location of neutral words. Change in this index from before to after training (pre minus post) thus reflected the extent to which training had led to greater avoidance of threat. This index was correlated with another index computed to reflect reduced mood response to stress (combining anxiety with depression scores) from before to after training, in all participants. There was a significant correlation between the two indices, $r(62) = 0.33$, $p < .05$. The relationship seemed stronger in the case of anxiety than depressed mood, $r(62) = .34, p < .01$ vs. $r(62) = .20$, n.s., although the correlations did not differ significantly. Thus, the extent to which participants reduced their attention to threatening words was modestly but significantly related to the degree of decreased emotional vulnerability to stress.

In the final phase of the present research, experiments 7 and 8 were designed to investigate the impact of several thousand training trials extended across many sessions, on responses to a real-life stress. In experiment 7, students were allocated to 10 sessions of training with a total of 7500 training trials, spread through the month prior to an examination. Unlike the previous experiments in which participants had anxiety scores in the normal range, students taking part in the last two experiments were selected on the basis of having elevated trait anxiety scores. Mean trait score of the total sample was 55 on the State-Trait Anxiety Inventory (STAI; Spielberger, Gorsuch, Lushene, Vagg, & Jacobs, 1983).

As before, for one group ($n = 15$) target probes consistently appeared in the prior location of nonthreatening words, thus discouraging attention to threatening information. Unlike previous experiments, however, there was no condition in which attention to threat was trained, partly for ethical reasons, and partly because attention to threat was likely to be present in any case in this highly anxious population, who were already under stress. Instead, in the other (control) condition ($n = 14$), targets appeared equally often in both locations throughout.

Test trials were included in the latter part of each session, with half (48) involving new word pairs presented for 500 ms, while in the other half new words were presented for only 16 ms before being masked. Analysis of performance in these test trials during the first (sessions 1–4) and second half (session 5–10) of training revealed the expected significant effects of training. Of particular interest, given the failure to find any effects of masked stimuli after one session of training in experiment 5, in the analysis of masked trials alone the group by time interaction approached significance, $p < .06$. In the second half of training, but not in the first, the group trained to avoid threat tended to be slower than the control group to detect targets in the location of threat words.

The trait scale of the STAI was used to assess change in vulnerability to anxiety across the whole training period. Although this scale is—by design—less variable over time than are measures of mood or state anxiety, it is in fact quite sensitive to the relatively slower reductions in vulnerability seen following cognitive-behavioural treatments (e.g., Borkovec & Costello, 1993). Analysis of trait anxiety scores obtained before and after training revealed a group by time interaction, $p < .01$, reflecting a decrease averaging just over 10 points in those trained to avoid threat words and no change in the control group. However, interpretation of this interaction was compromised by the fact that—due to random allocation—the latter group had lower mean scores than the attend threat group prior to training.

For this reason experiment 8 constituted a closely similar replication, but in which both groups were matched for trait anxiety scores at the outset (both means 51). In this experiment, students were again allocated to an "avoid threat" ($n = 16$) or to a control condition ($n = 14$), and trained over eight sessions within a three week period for a total of 6000 training trials.

As before, there were 96 noncontingent test trials in each session, now divided into old and new words, with presentation being either for 500 ms or 16 ms before being masked. Analysis of this critical masked condition with new words, and comparing across only the pre-training and final post-training occasions, revealed a significant group by time interaction, $p < .05$. The control group showed no change over the training period, but by session 8 the "avoid threat" training group had become less attentive to threatening than to neutral words, even when the words were presented under conditions of restricted awareness. In the analysis of trait anxiety scores from before training to after session 8, hypothesis-driven tests showed a significant reduction in trait anxiety for the group trained to avoid threat, $p < .05$, but no significant change in the control group.

We draw a number of important conclusions from these experiments. First, attention deployment tasks used previously to assess biases occurring naturally in anxious patients can be used experimentally to induce similar biases in the laboratory. Second, after extended training, parallel effects were sometimes seen for stimuli that had been masked to restrict awareness, suggesting that conscious monitoring may be unnecessary to maintain the induced bias. Third, and perhaps most important, the results suggest that processing bias can influence emotional vulnerability to stress, at least in the short term. We shall return to discussing the more general implications of these findings after describing related experiments on changing interpretation bias.

PROCEDURES FOR EXPERIMENTALLY INDUCING INTERPRETATIVE BIAS

Richards and French (1992) provided an elegant experimental demonstration that anxiety-prone individuals are more likely than their low anxious counterparts to adopt threatening interpretations of homographs. Homographs with threatening and nonthreatening meanings (e.g., growth) were presented as primes in a lexical decision task, followed by nonwords or words that were associates of one of the homograph meanings (e.g., plant, cancer). Anxiety-prone students were faster to identify threatening associates following a homograph prime, while a low anxious group was faster to identify neutral associates. The authors concluded that the groups differed in their access to the emotional meanings of ambiguous words.

In a series of experiments carried out at the Institute of Psychiatry, University of London, Grey and Mathews (2000) investigated whether similar effects could be induced in volunteers with trait anxiety scores in the normal range. The induction task used was designed to encourage or discourage access to threatening meanings of homographs that have both threatening and nonthreatening meanings. For example, in experiment 1, participants completed a word fragment completion task as quickly as they could, with each fragment preceded by a homograph that was to be used as a clue to the correct completion. Of the 120 words used as clues, a critical subset of 40 homographs had both threatening and nonthreatening meanings, as in the example below. Thus, the homograph "batter" could be followed either by a fragment corresponding to a neutral meaning, such as "p-nc-ke" (pancake), or by one corresponding to a threatening meaning, such as "ass--lt" (assault).

Volunteers were allocated at random to one of two training conditions (each n = 20). In the first, fragments following the critical homographs could be completed only by a word associated with their threatening meaning. In the second condition, the correct completion always corresponded to a nonthreatening meaning. After 120 "training" trials, participants continued without any obvious change in procedure to a set of 60 test trials. Of these 60 test trials, 40 were fillers and 20 included fragments matching either the threatening or non-threatening meaning of the preceding homographs, half of which had appeared before (old) and half of which had not (new).

For each training group, the critical 20 test items required threatening solutions for half of that group while the remaining half went on to items requiring nonthreatening solutions. Solution times for these critical items revealed a significant interaction of group by test valence by old/new homograph. After training with threat meanings, associates that were consistent with the practised valence were completed faster, regardless of whether the homographs were new or old. After nonthreat training however, this effect was significant only for old homographs.

Experiment 2 employed a similar method, but the number of critical training trials was doubled, and the test that followed was changed to a lexical decision task, as used by Richards and French (1992). In these test trials, old and new homographs were presented for 750 ms as primes, followed by word or nonword targets. The valence of word targets was a within-subject factor in this experiment, so that for all participants half of the words were associated with a threatening meaning of the homograph and half with a nonthreatening meaning.

In the analysis of these lexical decision latencies there was a significant interaction of group by threat/non-threat target in the expected direction, not significantly qualified by whether homographs were old or new. Divided by group, participants trained with threat meaning made faster decisions for all threat word targets, but in the other group the converse effect was again significant only for old homographs.

To test if these effects persisted under training conditions designed to discourage an active search for valenced meanings, experiment 3 essentially replicated experiment 2, but used a relatedness-judgement training task instead of word completion. In each training trial, a threatening or nonthreatening associate (depending on group assignment) was presented first, followed after 750 ms. by the relevant homograph. Participants were instructed to determine if the two words were related in meaning or not, and to respond as quickly as possible with a key press corresponding to "yes" or "no". For example, participants saw either the word "pancake" or "assault" first, and were then required to respond "yes" when the homograph "batter" followed. The intent of presenting the unambiguous associate *prior* to the homograph was to ensure that the required meaning was always accessed, and to remove any incentive to search for alternative meanings.

To assess training effects, the same lexical decision task used in experiment 2 was repeated. Both groups were significantly speeded when a target word matched the trained valence, and this was equally true for both old and new homographs. Thus the training effects in experiment 3 were at least as strong as those seen in experiment 2, despite removing the need to search for valenced meaning during training. This finding implies that active search is not required in order to induce an interpretative bias: Repeated practice in accessing one valence of meaning is sufficient.

Finally, to determine if negative training, positive training, or both, had significant effects, the groups described above were compared with a further baseline group given the same lexical decision task following exposure to a control condition not involving any of the critical homographs. Mean lexical decision latencies for threatening word targets were slowest for the positive trained groups, intermediate for the baseline group, and fastest for negative trained groups. This order was reversed for nonthreatening word targets. Thus, this comparison showed that both negative and positive training produced significant effects relative to an untrained baseline.

The conclusions to be drawn from this series are that, as with attention, a bias in the interpretation of ambiguous stimuli resembling that seen in anxiety-prone individuals can be induced by practice in accessing valenced meanings. Because in experiment 3 the effect extended to new homographs, which appeared in a novel task, it is clear that it does not depend simply on repeating the same responses made previously. Rather, it seems as if access to a whole class of valenced meanings was facilitated.

EFFECT OF INDUCED INTERPRETATIVE BIAS ON EMOTIONAL VULNERABILITY

A second series of experiments (Mathews & Mackintosh, 2000) extended these conclusions to the interpretation of texts describing realistic ambiguous social situations. In each experiment, community volunteers recruited at the Medical Research Council's Cognition and Brain Sciences Unit at Cambridge read about and imagined themselves in about 100 social situations that ended in an emotionally positive or negative outcome (training descriptions).

In experiment 1, at the end of each of these training descriptions, participants completed a word fragment (having only one solution) that resolved the meaning of the preceding text in either a positive or negative direction, depending on group assignment. Thus, one such description ended with the sentence "*Getting ready to go, you think that the new people you will meet will find you bor-ng/fri-ndly*". To further reinforce the assigned emotional resolution, a "comprehension" question followed that required an answer confirming or extending the valence of the imposed interpretation (e.g., "*Will you be disliked by your new acquaintances?*" with error feedback for an "incorrect" response).

After all of these training descriptions were completed, participants read 10 new test descriptions that remained ambiguous in emotional outcome and later gave recognition ratings for disambiguated versions of the final sentence from each test description. For example, one test description about giving a speech ended with the sentence "*As you speak, you notice some people in the audience start to laugh''*. Sample recognition items included *"As you speak, people in the audience laugh appreciatively"* and *"As you speak, people in the audience find your efforts laughable"*. As described earlier, Eysenck et al. (1991) had previously shown that a similar recognition task revealed differences in interpretation bias between anxious patients and controls.

Recognition ratings for the disambiguated test descriptions confirmed that the interpretations made were valenced in a direction consistent with the training received. The group allocated to negative meanings in training gave higher recognition ratings to threatening interpretations of the ambiguous descriptions than did the other group, and vice versa. Furthermore, scores on the state scale of the STAI showed significant changes in anxious mood across the experiment. The group trained to make negative interpretations reported increased anxiety while the positive trained group tended to report decreases.

In order to test the role of actively generating valenced meanings, the above procedure was repeated in experiment 2, but with the emotional outcome of each description integrated into the description itself. Thus, the previous example sentence was changed (with valence varied to match group assignment) to *"Getting ready to go, you think that the new people you will meet will find you boring (friendly). You will (not) be disliked by your new acquaintances"*. Word fragments and comprehension questions were again included but these were emotionally neutral and unrelated to the (already) valenced meaning. In the recognition test that followed exposure to ambiguous items as before, ratings once more differed significantly across groups, as in experiment 1, showing that an interpretative bias had been induced. Despite this, there was no trace of any anxiety differences induced by training between groups. Thus, although active search for and generation of meanings appeared to be unnecessary for the induction of interpretation bias itself, it was apparently critical in producing mood change.

A final experiment to be discussed here (experiment 5 in Mathews & Mackintosh, 2000), was designed to be a rigorous test of the hypothesis that active generation of meanings is critical to creating changes in anxious mood. In this experiment, the training procedure of experiment 2 involving passive exposure to positive or negative training descriptions was repeated, alongside two new conditions. These new conditions also began as in experiment 2, with descriptions that had positive or negative emotional outcomes already supplied, but then switched to interpolated blocks of ambiguous items. The outcome of these latter descriptions remained ambiguous to the end, but the "comprehension" question that followed forced readers to resolve the emotional outcome, albeit without determining the direction of that resolution. Thus, an ambiguous description of a friend not responding to your greeting in a crowded street ended with *"The reason that she did not answer is not difficult to guess"*, followed by the question *"Did she deliberately ignore your call to her in the street?"*. The point of this manipulation was to more closely resemble natural conditions in which the emotional meanings of real social situations often remain ambiguous but may then be actively resolved in a biased fashion.

The answers given to the supposed comprehension questions revealed that following prior exposure to negative descriptions, readers imposed negative interpretations on just over 50% of the ambiguous items, whereas following exposure to positive descriptions they did so in only about 20%. Generation of the intended valenced meanings of these ambiguous items was thus only partial, compared to 100% passive exposure to the designated valence in the comparison groups. Despite this, only the former groups demonstrated changes in anxiety, and these changes were very similar in form to those seen in the first experiment of this series.

In summary, biases in the interpretation of ambiguous information, resembling those seen in anxious patients (or in low anxious controls) were induced in unselected volunteers. These biases influenced the interpretation of new material which had not been previously exposed during training and which sometimes appeared in a new task context. In the second and final experiment described here, interpretation biases could be induced—as indexed by later recognition performance—despite absence of any measurable mood change. Most important for our present purposes is that change in state anxiety did not depend on the acquisition of interpretative bias *per se*, but on whether or not congruent emotional interpretations were actively generated by the participant (in the first and final experiment).

COGNITIVE MECHANISMS UNDERLYING THE INDUCTION OF PROCESSING BIASES

Despite the different induction methods involved, the conclusions to be drawn about attentional and interpretative biases are quite similar. Biases induced by practice in attending to valenced words, or by encoding valenced interpretations, extended to new exemplars not exposed during training. This finding appears to mimic the fairly general attentional and interpretative differences found between anxious patients and nonanxious controls. In both types of training, consistent access to valenced meanings was sufficient to induce a processing bias, but did not in itself produce any measurable changes in affect. Thus there were no changes in state anxiety before and after training to attend to or avoid threatening words; nor were there any changes after induction of an interpretative bias, provided that this did not involve active generation of emotional meanings.

We suggest that changes in anxiety occurred when—and only when—the processing of emotionally significant events was systematically biased. By ''emotionally significant'' we mean events that commonly elicit either negative or relatively more positive emotions, depending on how they are processed. We do not mean to imply that the critical events necessary to demonstrate emotional change were identical across all the experiments reviewed. These varied from a difficult anagram task or the anticipation of a real-life examination, to actively generating emotional interpretations related to oneself. We do propose, however, that the key feature common to these events is that the emotion they evoke depends on the valenced aspects or meanings that are selected for further processing. In the anagram task, for example, participants could focus on those items that were successfully solved, or on those that were not. In the active generation task, participants could select an interpretation, such as "My friend deliberately ignored me", or a more benign explanation. In both examples, mood effects would depend on the extent to which training influenced how the events were processed.

As well as providing common conclusions, the experiments also open up many similar questions. Among these are whether the induced biases can be attributed to demand effects, to unreported mood changes, to semantic priming or to learned production rules. We believe that demand effects can probably be ruled out, because in both types of induction we consistently observed systematic changes in the latency to detect neutral targets, to solve word fragments or make lexical decisions, that would be extremely difficult to simulate. When asked, all of those exposed to valenced texts denied that they had been influenced by the tasks they had practised. Perhaps most telling, after extended practice, there were measurable effects due to masked words of which participants were completely unaware.

It also seems improbable to us that undetected changes in mood could have been responsible for the changes in bias, rather than vice versa. In most experiments, we obtained ratings of mood on several occasions, both before and after bias was induced, whether by attending to valenced words or by passively reading about valenced outcomes. In each case, no detectable changes in mood occurred. However, the same measures were quite sensitive to the effects of mild laboratory stress, and to the active generation of valenced meanings, both of which led to significant mood changes. Furthermore, passive exposure and active generation elicited the same interpretative bias—as assessed by recognition measures—yet very different patterns of mood change. Thus there is nothing in the induction procedure *per se* that produced change in affect, and we are forced to the conclusion that such changes only follow the *active deployment* of a processing bias, rather than the reverse.

A more difficult question is whether we can attribute the acquisition of bias to semantic priming of valenced content, or to a learned production rule in the selection of valenced meanings. The former explanation implies that repeated attention to valenced words or text primes the whole domain of meanings consistent with that valence. Then, when related novel exemplars are encountered later they are also more easily activated, due to shared associative links, increasing their chances of being attended to or encoded. Alternatively, it could be that selecting a valenced meaning during training strengthens those processes required to make similar selections later. This could be thought of as an implicit production rule taking the following form: If two valenced alternatives are present, then select the negative (or positive) one. There is not sufficient evidence at present to choose one of these explanations over the other. However, we offer below a theoretical view in which the induction process is modelled within a system containing elements of both the priming and learned production rule explanations.

Whatever the mechanism involved, it remains uncertain whether induced biases are really the same as those occurring naturally in clinically anxious patients. The biases induced in most of the studies described here are likely to be very transient compared with those occurring naturally. However, naturally occurring biases are also known to be sensitive to short-term stress (e.g., MacLeod & Mathews, 1988; Mogg, Mathews, Bird, & MacGregor-Morris, 1990) and can be eliminated by treatment (e.g., Mathews, Mogg, Kentish, & Eysenck, 1995; Mogg, Bradley, Millar, & White, 1995). Furthermore, the experiments described earlier suggest that repeated attentional training sessions may be able to reduce anxiety scores on measures often taken as indicating durable tendencies. Further research is clearly needed before this question can be resolved.

ACCOUNTING FOR THE EMOTIONAL EFFECTS OF INDUCED ATTENTIONAL BIAS

Earlier in this paper we described a model intended to provide an account of attentional and interpretative bias in anxiety. In neither this, nor alternative views (see Mathews & Mackintosh, 1998, for a review), was there any provision for how such biases can be induced, and whether or how they might influence proneness to anxiety. In the final part of this paper, we attempt to provide such an account.

In our model, output from a threat evaluation system is supposed to selectively activate representations of potential threats, thus facilitating attention to their location. Although we assume that this nonconscious system evolved to allow the rapid detection of perceptual cues predicting likely dangers (heights, snakes, and so on), there is also evidence that information about new conditioned stimuli can be acquired by this system through learning (LeDoux, 1995). We have argued that this same process might allow the nonconscious evaluation system to respond to certain valenced words, sufficient to cause orienting responses or cognitive interference. Supporting evidence includes Stroop interference from masked emotional words (Williams et al., 1996), skin conductance responses to masked phobia-related words (van den Hout et al., 2000) and masked priming effects on affective decisions for words when the masked prime has itself been recently evaluated for valence (Abrams & Greenwald, 2000).

However, none of this evidence shows that the nonconscious system typically evaluates words as a real threat, sufficient to elicit emotion. In our own extensive experience as readers, threatening words do not often result in actual feelings of fear. One exception may be provided by studies in which panic disorder patients sometimes experienced panic attacks when reading aloud word pairs closely associated with their worst fears (e.g., palpitations—coronary; choking—suffocation, see Clark et al., 1988). We suppose this could happen if certain words directly evoke memories, images or bodily sensations that match events previously associated with fear. Similarly, phobic or PTSD patients often experience anxiety when they are asked to imagine themselves in feared situations as part of cognitive-behavioural treatment. Presumably this occurs because the representations corresponding to such evoked images provide a close match with information already encoded within the threat evaluation system. Because the threat evaluation system is supposed to have evolved prior to the development of language, we suppose that it is likely to be more responsive to information encoded in sensory or perceptual form than to words encoded only as lexical representations.

Let us now consider the case in which individuals (not selected as being highly vulnerable to anxiety) were trained with targets consistently appearing in the location of negative words. The latency of decisions about whether a word is positive or negative does not vary with anxiety (Mathews & Milroy, 1994), and most people make them easily and rapidly. Consequently, we suppose that knowledge of word valence can be accessed from lexical or semantic memory, without necessarily involving the nonconscious threat evaluation system. Attending to words having a negative valence will be reinforced by the consequent efficient detection of targets. With practice this should prime or even partially automate the cognitive procedures involved in selectively attending to lexical representations having negative valence. After extended practice, this may lead to attentional effects even in response to the attenuated signal provided by masked words. As indicated earlier, however, we assume that, under normal circumstances, lexical representations alone are unlikely to elicit a significant response from the threat evaluation system, and attending to words should thus not be associated with changes in anxiety.

After training, the same individuals were exposed to a stressful task. Any negative thoughts that were cued (e.g., about failure) should again be preferentially attended, due to the prior practice with similar lexical information. In this case, however, attention to negative self-referent thoughts is likely to promote access to other associated autobiographical memories or images. Because the form in which such information is encoded can elicit a greater response from the threat evaluation system than valenced words, it is more likely to be evaluated as a threat and trigger increases in anxiety.

By the same token, when being trained to avoid threat words, paying attention to nonthreatening words will result in more efficient performance.

Again, access to the lexical valence of the presented words would be sufficient to allow rejection of words having negative meanings. In this case,
the cognitive procedures involved in selecting words without negative meanings, or those involved in inhibiting attention to words with negative meanings, will become primed or partially automated. When later faced with the
stress task, although thoughts about task failure may still occur, the prior
practice in avoiding related information should ensure that attention to such
negative meanings will not be maintained, or is inhibited. This should in
turn prevent the production of associated memories or images encoded in a
form that elicits a significant response from the threat evaluation system,
and will correspondingly decrease the chances of any resultant anxiety
increase.

ACCOUNTING FOR THE EMOTIONAL EFFECTS OF INDUCED INTERPRETATIVE BIAS

Unlike the effects of training attention, state anxiety did change under some
conditions of interpretation training. In the passive exposure condition, however, the effects were similar to those that occurred in the attentional training
described above. That is, we suppose that the cognitive processes involved in
selecting one valence of text meanings will be primed, and with prolonged
practice may be partially automated. Then, when encountering new ambiguous
texts, access to the practised valence will be facilitated and the resultant interpretation encoded for later recognition. As in the case of selective attention to
words, valenced text meanings are unlikely to provide a sufficient match with
representations in the threat evaluation system as to elicit anxiety state
changes.

In contrast, actively generating emotional interpretations during training
produced both biased encoding *and* congruent changes in reported affect. As
with passive exposure, we assume that repeated generation of valenced meanings of text during training will prime the cognitive processes involved in
accessing and selecting congruent interpretations. However, the type of information that readers must access in order to generate emotional meanings is
qualitatively different from that required when just passively reading text. In
order to complete the disambiguating word fragments and answer questions
about how they would feel, subjects must construct or reconstitute internal
models of themselves in the emotional situations described, presumably drawing
on images or memories of related events. This type of processing is likely to
utilise information in a form matching that of representations in the threat
evaluation system. Consequently, and in contrast to passive reading, active
generation of emotional meaning is likely to result in a congruent change in
emotional state.

CONCLUSIONS

We have argued that previous evidence on emotional processing biases has been equally consistent with causal or noncausal views. On this past evidence, biases could cause vulnerability to anxiety, biases could be a by-product of such vulnerability, or both may be brought about by another variable, such that neither causes the other. In contrast, we believe that the experiments described here offer the most convincing evidence to date that specific processing biases can play a causal role in the development of vulnerability to anxiety. Furthermore, we claim that the data show that our induction procedures do not necessarily produce emotion in themselves, but that it is only when induced biases are deployed in the processing of emotionally significant information that they elicit anxiety. Finally, we have proposed a tentative theoretical account of the way in which induction methods work, consistent with existing cognitive and neuroscience research.

Our data do not allow us to argue that the reverse direction of causation might not also operate: nor would we wish to. It seems quite likely that state anxiety or related contextual influences can induce processing biases. Indeed, the very effectiveness of our induction procedures suggests that processing biases are anything but fixed, and can presumably be learned and unlearned, and come under the control of both environmental and state variables. However, we attach special significance to the finding that manipulating processing bias can cause changes in vulnerability to anxiety, not only because it advances theoretical understanding of causation, but also because it may have implications for treatment and prevention. Research into the optimal methods for inducing benign processing biases could conceivably contribute to the development of more efficient cognitive treatments, or more effective methods of preventing excessive anxiety.

Manuscript received 14 November 2000
Revised manuscript received 18 April 2001

REFERENCES

Abrams, R.L., & Greenwald, A.G. (2000). Parts outweigh the whole (word) in unconscious analysis of meaning. *Psychological Science, 11*, 118–124.

Borkovec, T.D., & Costello, E. (1993). Efficacy of applied relaxation and cognitive-behavioral therapy in the treatment of generalised anxiety disorder. *Journal of Consulting and Clinical Psychology, 61*, 611–619.

Bush, G., Luu, P., & Posner, M.I. (2000). Cognitive and emotional influences in anterior cingulate cortex. *Trends in Cognitive Sciences, 4*, 215–222.

Bryne, A., & Eysenck, M.W. (1995). Trait anxiety, anxious mood, and threat detection. *Cognition and Emotion, 9*, 549–562.

Compton, R. (2000) Ability to disengage attention predicts negative affect. *Cognition and Emotion, 14*, 401–415.

Drevets, W.C., & Raichle, M.E. (1998). Reciprocal suppression of regional cerebral blood flow during emotional versus higher cognitive processes: Implications for interactions between emotion and cognition. *Cognition and Emotion*, *12*, 353–385.

Eysenck, M.W., Mogg, K., May, J., Richards, A., & Mathews, A. (1991). Bias in interpretation of ambiguous sentences related to threat in anxiety. *Journal of Abnormal Psychology*, *100*, 144–50.

Fox, E., Russo, R., Bowles, R., & Dutton, K. (2001). Do threatening stimuli draw or hold visual attention in subclinical anxiety? *Journal of Experimental Psychology: General*, *130*, 681–700.

Grey, S., & Mathews, A. (2000). Effects of training on interpretation of emotional ambiguity. *Quarterly Journal of Experimental Psychology*, *53*, 1143–1162.

Hirsch, C., & Mathews, A. (1997). Interpretative inferences when reading about emotional events. *Behaviour Research and Therapy*, *35*, 1123–1132.

Hirsch, C., & Mathews, A. (2000). Impaired positive inferential bias in social phobia. *Journal of Abnormal Psychology*, *109*, 705–712.

Kalin, N.H., Shelton, S.E., Davidson, R.J., & Kelley, A.E. (2001). The primate amygdala mediates acute fear but not the behavioral and physiological components of anxious temperament. *Journal of Neuroscience*, *21*, 2067–2074.

Lang, P.J., Bradley, M.M., Fitzsimmons, J.R., Cuthbert, B.N., Scott, J.D., Moulder, B., & Nangia, V. (1998). Emotional arousal and activation of the visual cortex: an fMRI analysis. *Psychophysiology*, *35*, 199–210.

LeDoux, J.E. (1995). Emotion: clues from the brain. *Annual Review of Psychology*, *46*, 209–235.

MacDonald, A.W., Cohen, J.D., Stenger, V.A., & Carter, C.S. (2000). Dissociating the role of the dorsolateral prefrontal and anterior cingulate cortex in cognitive control. *Science*, *288*, 1835–1838.

MacLeod, C., & Hagan, R. (1992). Individual differences in the selective processing of threatening information, and emotional responses to a stressful life event. *Behaviour Research and Therapy*, *30*, 151–561.

MacLeod, C., & Mathews, A. (1988). Anxiety and the allocation of attention to threat. *Quarterly Journal of Experimental Psychology*, *40*, 653–670.

MacLeod, C., & Mathews, A. (1991). Biased cognitive operations in anxiety: Accessibility of information or assignment of processing priorities? *Behaviour Research and Therapy*, *29*, 599–610.

MacLeod, C., Mathews, A., & Tata, C. (1986). Attentional bias in emotional disorders. *Journal of Abnormal Psychology*, *95*, 15–20.

MacLeod, C., & Rutherford, E.M. (1992). Anxiety and the selective processing of emotional information: mediating roles of awareness, trait and state variables, and personal relevance of stimulus materials. *Behaviour Research and Therapy*, *30*, 479–91.

MacLeod, C., Rutherford, E.M., Campbell, L., Ebsworthy, G., & Holker, L. (in press). Selective attention and emotional vulnerability: assessing the causal basis of their association through the experimental induction of attentional bias. *Journal of Abnormal Psychology*.

Mansell, W., Clark, D.M., Ehlers, A., & Chen, Y.P. (1999) Social anxiety and attention away from emotional faces, *Cognition and Emotion*, *13*, 673–690.

Mathews, A., & Mackintosh, B. (1998). A cognitive model of selective processing in anxiety. *Cognitive Therapy and Research*, *22*, 539–560.

Mathews, A., & Mackintosh, B. (2000). Induced emotional interpretation bias and anxiety. *Journal of Abnormal Psychology*, *109*, 602–615.

Mathews, A., Mackintosh, B., & Fulcher, E. (1997). Cognitive biases in anxiety and attention to threat. *Trends in Cognitive Science*, *1*, 340–345.

Mathews, A., May, J., Mogg, K., & Eysenck, M. (1990). Attentional bias in anxiety: selective search or defective filtering? *Journal of Abnormal Psychology*, *99*, 166–173.

Mathews, A., & MacLeod, C. (1994). Cognitive approaches to emotion and emotional disorders. *Annual Review of Psychology*, *45*, 25–50.

Mathews, A., & Milroy, R. (1994). Processing of emotional meaning in anxiety. *Cognition and Emotion, 8*, 535–553.

Mathews, A., Mogg, K., Kentish, J., & Eysenck, M. (1995). Effect of psychological treatment on cognitive bias in generalised anxiety disorder. *Behaviour Research and Therapy, 33*, 293–303.

Mogg, K., & Bradley, B.P. (1998). A cognitive-motivational analysis of anxiety. *Behaviour Research and Therapy, 36*, 809–848.

Mogg, K., & Bradley, B.P. (1999). Some methodological issues in assessing attentional biases for threatening faces in anxiety: a replication study using a modified version of the probe detection task. *Behaviour Research and Therapy, 37*, 595–604.

Mogg, K., Bradley, B.P., Millar, N., & White, J. (1995) A follow-up study of cognitive bias in generalised anxiety disorder. *Behaviour Research and Therapy, 33*, 927–935.

Mogg, K., Bradley, B.P., Williams, R., & Mathews, A. (1993). Subliminal processing of emotional information in anxiety and depression. *Journal of Abnormal Psychology, 102*, 1–8.

Mogg, K., Mathews, A., Bird, C., & Macgregor-Morris, R. (1990). Effects of stress and anxiety on the processing of threat stimuli. *Journal of Personality and Social Psychology, 59*, 1230–1237.

Mogg, K., Mathews, A., Eysenck, M., & May, J. (1991). Biased cognitive operations in anxiety: Artefact, processing priorities or attentional search? *Behaviour Research and Therapy, 29*, 459–467.

Öhman, A., & Soares, J.J.F. (1994). Unconscious anxiety: phobic responses to masked stimuli. *Journal of Abnormal Psychology, 103*, 231–240.

Öhman, A., & Soares, J.J.F. (1998). Emotional conditioning to masked stimuli: expectancies for aversive outcomes following nonrecognized fear-relevant stimuli. *Journal of Experimental Psychology: General, 127*, 69–82.

Richards, A., & French, C.C. (1992). An anxiety-related bias in semantic activation when processing threat/neutral homographs. *Quarterly Journal of Experimental Psychology, 45*, 503–25.

Rolls, E.T. (1999). *The brain and emotion.* New York: Oxford University Press.

Spielberger, C.D., Gorsuch, R.L., Lushene, R., Vagg, P.R., & Jacobs, G.A. (1983). *Manual for the State-Trait Anxiety Inventory.* Palo Alto, CA: Consulting Psychologists Press.

Van den Hout, M.A. de Jong, P., & Kindt, M. (2000). Masked fear words produce increased SCRs: an anomaly for Öhman's theory of pre-attentive processing in anxiety. *Psychophysiology, 37*, 283–288.

Williams, J.M.G., Mathews, A., & MacLeod, C. (1996). The emotional Stroop task and psychopathology. *Psychological Bulletin, 120*, 3–24.

Williams, M., MacLeod, C., Watts, F., & Mathews, A. (1997). *Cognitive psychology and emotional disorders,* Wiley: London.

Yiend, J., & Mathews, A. (2001). Anxiety and attention to threatening pictures. *Quarterly Journal of Experimental Psychology, 54A*, 665–681.

COGNITION AND EMOTION, 2002, *16* (3), 355–379

Attentional bias for threat: Evidence for delayed disengagement from emotional faces

Elaine Fox, Riccardo Russo, and Kevin Dutton

University of Essex, Colchester, UK

The present paper reports three new experiments suggesting that the valence of a face cue can influence attentional effects in a cueing paradigm. Moreover, heightened trait anxiety resulted in increased attentional dwell-time on emotional facial stimuli, relative to neutral faces. Experiment 1 presented a cueing task, in which the cue was either an "angry", "happy", or "neutral" facial expression. Targets could appear either in the same location as the face (valid trials) or in a different location to the face (invalid trials). Participants did not show significant variations across the different cue types (angry, happy, neutral) in responding to a target on *valid* trials. However, the valence of the face did affect response times on *invalid* trials. Specifically, participants took longer to respond to a target when the face cue was "angry" or "happy" relative to neutral. In Experiment 2, the cue-target stimulus onset asynchrony (SOA) was increased and an overall *inhibition of return* (IOR) effect was found (i.e., *slower* responses on valid trials). However, the "angry" face cue eliminated the IOR effect for both high and low trait anxious groups. In Experiment 3, threat-related and jumbled facial stimuli reduced the magnitude of IOR for high, but not for low, trait-anxious participants. These results suggest that: (i) attentional bias in anxiety may reflect a difficulty in disengaging from threat-related and emotional stimuli, and (ii) threat-related and ambiguous cues can influence the magnitude of the IOR effect.

Many theories of attention assume that one of the primary functions of attentional mechanisms is to facilitate fast and accurate perception of objects appearing in the visual scene (e.g., Yantis, 1996). Likewise, a primary function of the basic emotion of *fear* is considered to be the facilitation of the detection of danger in the environment (e.g., LeDoux, 1996). It should not, therefore, be too surprising to find a close association between the brain mechanisms underlying

Correspondence should be addressed to Dr Elaine Fox, Department of Psychology, University of Essex, Wivenhoe Park, Colchester CO4 3SQ, UK; email: efox@essex.ac.uk

The research reported here was supported by a project grant from the Wellcome Trust to Elaine Fox and Riccardo Russo (Ref: 045800/Z/95/Z). Some of the data presented in Experiment 3 was collected by Louisa Glenn as part of an undergraduate research project under the supervision of Elaine Fox.

http://www.tandf.co.uk/journals/pp/02699931.html   DOI:10.1080/02699930143000527

attention and those underlying fear. Many psychological theories have examined attentional processing in people with disorders of the fear system (i.e., anxiety disorders) and concluded that attentional biases do play an important role in the etiology and maintenance of anxiety disorders (e.g., Eysenck, 1992; Mathews & MacLeod, 1994; Williams, Watts, MacLeod, & Matthews, 1988, 1997). Moreover, psychobiological research has shown that fear responses may well be driven by the pre-attentive analysis of stimuli as being threat-related (e.g., snakes, angry facial expressions), and that these mechanisms may then result in an automatic shift of attentional resources to the location of the threatening object (Öhman, 1993; Öhman & Soares, 1993).

Experimental psychological research has added to the evidence that anxious individuals may be especially sensitive to the presence of threat-related objects in their environment. Findings characteristic of such research are those which have emanated from modifications of the probe detection task. This task was designed to measure the allocation of spatial attention, and typically shows that participants tend to be faster in detecting a probe if it occurs in an attended, rather than an unattended, location on a computer screen (Navon & Margalit, 1983). MacLeod, Mathews, and Tata (1986) modified this paradigm by presenting a pair of words 5 cm apart for 500 ms, followed by a probe to be detected in either the upper or lower location on a subset of trials. The interesting trials were those in which one of the words was threat-related and the other neutral. The results showed that patients with generalised anxiety disorder (GAD) were faster to detect a probe when it occurred in the location recently occupied by a threat-related word, in comparison with normal control participants. Subsequent research has used a target categorisation task with the probe paradigm such that participants were required to determine whether two dots were vertically (:) or horizontally (..) aligned. As before, the dots could appear either to the left or the right of fixation. However, unlike the traditional dot-detection task in which a number of trials with no target probe (catch trials) were necessary, this method allows all trials to be used giving a greater degree of statistical power. Using photographs of neutral, happy, and angry facial expressions previous research has found that participants with high levels of self-reported trait anxiety were faster when the probe was preceded by an angry, relative to a neutral, facial expression, and this pattern did not occur in participants' with low levels of self-reported trait anxiety (Bradley, Mogg, Falla, & Hamilton, 1998). Similar findings have also been found with photographs of fearful, relative to neutral, facial expressions (Fox, 2001). Thus, a growing literature using the dot-probe task with both words (e.g., Fox, 1993; MacLeod & Mathews, 1988; Mogg, Bradley, & Hallowel, 1994), and faces (Bradley et al., 1998; Fox, 2001) has led to the assumption that anxious people are biased in the initial orientation of attentive resources towards threat-related stimuli.

However, this interpretation of the pattern of results observed in the probe detection task has recently been challenged. Fox, Russo, Bowles, and Dutton (in press) have argued that the presence of threat-related stimuli may affect the *attentional dwell-time* or the ability to *disengage* attentional resources from threatening stimuli in anxious people. They pointed out that in the probe-detection task, because both locations are task-relevant, and presentation times are relatively long (*c.* 500 ms), participants may attend alternately to both locations and then continue to dwell on threat-related stimuli once they have been detected. If this indeed were the case, it would become virtually impossible to distinguish between differences in initial orienting and differences in attentional dwell time using the traditional probe detection task. A task more conducive to investigating disengage mechanisms is one in which a threat-related or neutral cue is presented alone for a very *brief* period in one of two possible locations. A target can then appear in either validly cued locations (i.e., cue and target appear in the same location) or invalidly cued locations (i.e., cue and target appear in different locations). It should be noted, however, that this task cannot measure enhanced attentional *orienting* towards a threat stimulus. Because only one stimulus is presented prior to the probe on each trial, any individual difference in the tendency to initially prioritise the assignment of attention to an emotional class of stimuli relative to another class of stimuli will not manifest itself on this task. Only effects that reflect differential disengagement of attention from alternative emotional stimulus classes will be revealed. Thus, the aim of the present research is to investigate differences in attentional disengagement from different emotional stimuli. The *invalid* trials are critical since reaction times can be compared following neutral, positive, and threat-related cues, giving a fairly direct measure of disengagement from threatening stimuli. If attentional dwell time increases in anxious people for threat-related stimuli then anxious people should be *slower* in detecting a target on *invalid* trials following a threat-related cue, relative to a positive or neutral cue. In a series of experiments using both schematic facial expressions, and photographs of real facial expressions, this predicted pattern of results was observed. Individuals with high levels of self-reported state anxiety took longer to respond to a target on invalid trials when the cue had been an angry facial expression. This pattern was not apparent in those with low levels of state anxiety (Fox et al., in press). Such results support the possibility that the probe-detection task may be a reflection of enhanced attentional dwell-time on threat-related stimuli, rather than or in addition to a reflection of facilitated orienting towards threatening stimuli.

One of the unexpected results of our earlier studies (Fox et al., in press) was the finding that state-anxiety rather than trait-anxiety was the main predictor of increased dwell-time on threat-related stimuli. We argued that state anxiety may represent a purer activation of the fear detection system of the brain and that therefore elevations of state anxiety might more strongly influence attention effects. Nevertheless, several cognitive theories of emotion predict that variations in trait anxiety should be associated with variations in attentional bias (e.g., Eysenck, 1997; Williams et al., 1997). We would also expect that the ability to disengage from threat-related stimuli should be related to an indivi-dual's level of trait anxiety. A recent study is of particular interest in this context. Yiend and Mathews (in press) presented an attentional task somewhat similar to the cueing paradigm used by Fox et al. (in press). Yiend and Mathews (in press) found that when pictures were used as location cues, high trait anxious participants were slower than low trait anxious controls when responding to targets requiring attentional disengagement from threat. Like Fox et al., they also concluded that attentional bias involves a specific difficulty in disengaging attention from the location of potential threat. However, whereas one study found that this effect was primarily related to the level of state anxiety (Fox et al., in press), the other found that trait anxiety was the better predictor (Yiend & Mathews, in press).

Thus, the aim of the present experiments was to further investigate the *enhanced dwell-time* hypothesis, and to determine whether the delay in disen-gaging from the location of threat is affected by an individual's level of trait anxiety. General theories of emotion and attention (e.g., Armony & LeDoux, 2000; LeDoux, 1996; Öhman, 1993) would suggest, of course, that threatening stimuli should influence attentional processing in a fairly general way. Thus, we can hypothesise that participants will show a general tendency to dwell on threatening stimuli, but that this tendency might be further increased by elevated trait anxiety. Experiment 1 is a close replication of a previous experiment (Fox et al., in press: experiment 3). However, in the previous experiment we pre-sented a target localisation task, such that the participant had to press either a left or a right-hand side button according to the *location* of a target (left or right) on the computer screen. One potential problem with this task is that the cue might directly activate a *response* (left or right) and therefore a motor preparation effect rather than an attentional effect might have produced the observed pattern of results (see Fox et al., in press, for further discussion). Moreover, a further problem with a location-based response is that, in principle, the information required to identify the probe location exists equally in both possible screen locations, rather than only in the location of the probe itself. Thus, a response could be made by simply attending to one side of the screen and making a ''presence/absence'' response. For these reasons, in the current experiment we presented a target categorisation task such that participants had to press one key if the target was a square and another key if the target was a circle. This change is important as any cue validity effects (i.e., faster responses on valid relative to invalid trials) cannot now be attributed to response preparation effects because the location of the cue (left or right) is not associated with the correct response (circle or square). In addition, information required to make the appropriate response can only be obtained by processing the probe itself in a probe categorisation task.

The primary aim of the current series of experiments was to further investigate whether attentional dwell-time increases when threatening facial expressions are presented as cues and whether this pattern is especially apparent in high trait anxious people. This can be measured on invalid trials when there is a short temporal lag between the cue and the target (e.g., Fox et al., in press). Experiments 2 and 3 both used the *inhibition of return* (IOR) paradigm (Posner & Cohen, 1984) to further investigate the enhanced dwell-time hypothesis. The task used was similar to that used in Experiment 1, except that the cue-target asynchrony was increased. IOR is the demonstration that target detection takes *longer* following a validly cued trial, relative to an invalidly cued trial, when the cue-target onset asynchrony is greater than about 600 ms. Posner and Cohen (1984) argued that IOR reflected a mechanism that served to favour novelty in visual scanning. In other words, visual attention is *inhibited* from returning to an already searched location, thus biasing the visual system towards "new" information. The mechanism proposed to underlie this pattern of early facilitation giving way to inhibition is as follows: (i) attention moves to the location of the cue; (ii) after a certain amount of time (e.g., > 300 ms) attention drifts back to a central location; and then (iii) attention is inhibited from returning to the initial location. If this sequence is correct then the IOR paradigm provides a unique test of the proposed disengage hypothesis. The logic is that if angry facial expressions are particularly effective in holding visual attention (i.e., increasing dwell-time), then IOR should be substantially reduced with these stimuli, or at least should be apparent over a longer time scale than that observed for neutral stimuli. Thus, three new experiments are reported to further test the enhanced dwell-time (or delayed disengagement) hypothesis as outlined by Fox et al. (in press).

EXPERIMENT 1

The aim of Experiment 1 was to replicate the findings of Fox et al. (in press: experiment 3) with a cueing paradigm that required a categorisation response. In our previous studies, a cue was presented to the left or right of fixation and the participant had to *localise* a target that could appear in either the left or right location. The key difference in the present study, however (the cue again appearing to the left or right of fixation), is that the target comprises either a square or a circle which the participant must *categorise* by pressing an appropriate key. The prediction is that participants will take longer to respond to a target on *invalid* trials when the cue is an angry facial expression, relative to when the cue is a happy or a neutral facial expression. This pattern is expected to be stronger for high trait anxious relative to low trait anxious people.

Method

Participants.   These were 34 undergraduate students from the University of Essex campus community ranging in age from 18 to 32 years with a modal age in the 20s. Those scoring at or above a score of 40 ($n = 21$) on the State Trait Anxiety Inventory (STAI; Spielberger, Gorsuch, Lushene, Vagg, & Jacobs,

1983) and those scoring at or below 35 ($n = 13$) were classified as high and low trait anxious participants, respectively. In various previous samples tested at the University of Essex we have found that the median on the Spielberger trait anxiety scale is 37. Therefore, in this and subsequent experiments we excluded people scoring between 35 and 40 in order to exclude those scoring near the median. These cut-offs should give us more statistical power by strengthening the independent variable of trait anxiety. Each participant had normal or corrected-to-normal eyesight and took part in one experimental session lasting about 45 minutes for which they received payment of £4.00.

Materials and procedure. Schematic faces were created by assembling standardised facial features in a computerised drawing package. There were three main face types: neutral, happy, and angry as shown in Figure 1. These faces have been used in our previous research (see Fox et al., in press). Each of the faces was 2.5 cm in height and 1.8 cm wide on the computer screen. The face stimuli were used as cues in the experiment. The target that participants had to categorise was either a white square with a diameter of 0.3 cm, or a white circle with a diameter of 0.3 cm. Cue and target stimuli were presented inside two dark grey boxes that were 5.3 cm high and 3.0 cm wide and were displayed 2.0 cm to the left and right of the central fixation point (cross shape). These boxes were continuously present on the computer screen. All stimuli were presented on a Pentium P5/120 PC with a 28 cm colour monitor and ATI Mach64 graphics card. All stimulus presentation and data collection was controlled by MEL software Version 2 (Schneider, 1988).

Early in the academic year, participants completed the STAI in a group testing session. On arrival at the laboratory toward the end of the academic year (about five weeks prior to examinations), each participant once again completed the STAI state anxiety scale, which gave a measure of state anxiety at test. On completion of the questionnaires, participants were asked to move to a computer in the same room for the reaction time experiment, where they

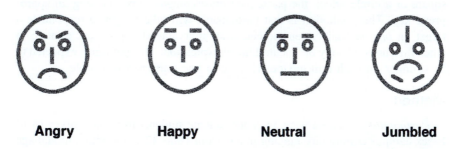

Angry   **Happy**   **Neutral**   **Jumbled**

Figure 1.   Example of schematic faces used in Experiments 1, 2, and 3. The jumbled face consisted of features of the ''angry'' face and was used in Experiment 3.

were seated about 50 cm from the computer monitor. The participant's task was to categorise the target that appeared in either the left or right hand location by pressing the "z" key for square and the "/" key for circle on a standard computer keyboard. Participants had to remember these response assignments which were not marked on the keyboard. The response assignments were reversed for half of the participants. The cue display consisted of one of the faces being presented in the upper half of either the left or the right box. The target (square or circle) later appeared in the lower half of either the left or the right box. This was to prevent any forward masking of the target by the face cue. The sequence of events within each trial was as follows. A fixation point (X) was presented at the centre of the screen for 1000 ms. A face cue was then presented in one of the peripheral boxes for 250 ms. The cue was then blanked out and 50 ms later the target (square or circle) was presented in the lower half of either the left or the right box until the participant responded (or until 2000 ms elapsed). This gave a cue-target onset asynchrony of 300 ms. There was an intertrial interval of 1000 ms.

Each participant completed 30 practice trials, followed by 240 experimental trials, divided into four blocks of 60. Three-quarters (75%) of the experimental trials (180) were valid (i.e., the target appeared in the same spatial location as the cue), and one-quarter (60) were invalid (i.e., the target appeared in the opposite spatial location to the cue). Neutral, happy, and angry face cues appeared 60 times each on valid trials and 20 times each on invalid trials. The probability of any particular cue appearing in the left- and right-handside boxes was equal. Thus, each type of cue was presented 80 times in the experimental trials: 40 times on the right (30 valid, 10 invalid) and 40 times on the left (30 valid, 10 invalid). Each target type (square or circle) appeared equally often in each condition of the experiment. The trials were presented in a different random order for each participant. Participants were told that the face cue would predict the location of the subsequent target on most (75%) trials, but they were told to try and keep their eyes focused on the centre of the screen and to respond as quickly and as accurately as possible.

Design.   A 2 (Anxiety: high and low trait anxiety) × 2 (Cue Validity: valid and invalid) × 3 (Cue Valence: neutral, happy, angry) ANOVA factorial design was used. Trait anxiety was a between-subjects factor while Cue Validity and Cue Valence were within-subjects factors. The main prediction was an Anxiety × Cue Validity X Cue Valence interaction such that cue validity effects (i.e., faster RTs on valid relative to invalid trials) should be *larger* on angry face trials than on either neutral or happy face trials. This larger validity effect is expected to be due to *slower* RTs on *invalid* angry face trials rather than to faster RTs on valid angry face trials. This pattern is expected to be particularly strong for high trait anxious participants.

Results

As shown in Table 1, the high trait anxious group scored significantly higher on measures of state anxiety compared to the low trait anxious group. A mixed design 2 (Anxiety: high and low trait anxiety) × 2 (Time of Testing: state anxiety at baseline and test) ANOVA revealed a significant main effect for the Trait Anxiety group, $F(1, 32) = 9.54$, $MS_e = 177.9$, $p < .004$, such that the high trait anxious participants had higher state anxiety scores than the low trait anxious participants. No other effects were significant.

Incorrect responses ($< 3.5\%$ of trials) and RT latencies of between 150 ms or above 1200 ms were eliminated from the data. The mean correct RT data are shown in Figure 2. In this and subsequent experiments, we report values for the Pillais multivariate test of significance (exact F-test) whenever the sphericity assumption was violated in univariate tests involving within-subjects factors. The RT data were subjected to a 2 (Anxiety: high and low trait anxiety) × 2 (Cue Validity: valid and invalid) × 3 (Cue Valence: neutral, happy, angry) ANOVA with participants as a random factor. There were main effects for Cue Validity, $F(1, 32) = 240.3$, $MS_e = 738.7$, $p < .001$, and for Cue Valence, Pillais $F(2, 31) = 4.12$, $p < .026$. Of greater theoretical importance, there was a significant Cue Validity × Cue Valence interaction, *Pillais* $F(2, 31) = 4.44$,

TABLE 1

Mean trait and state anxiety scores at baseline (B) and at testing (T), with (standard deviations), for high and low trait anxious participants in each of the three experiments

	High anxious	Low anxious	t
Experiment 1			
n	21	13	
Trait anxiety	47 (5)	29 (4)	
State anxiety (B)	39 (10)	28 (9)	3.2**
State anxiety (T)	41 (12)	31 (10)	2.6*
Experiment 2			
n	25	23	
Trait anxiety	50 (6)	31 (4)	
State anxiety (T)	45 (10)	27 (4)	7.8***
Experiment 3			
n	43	37	
Trait anxiety	52 (8)	29 (4)	
State anxiety (B)	39 (10)	32 (5)	3.9***
State anxiety (T)	47 (8)	33 (4)	9.7***

$*p < .05$; $**p < .01$; $***p < .001$.

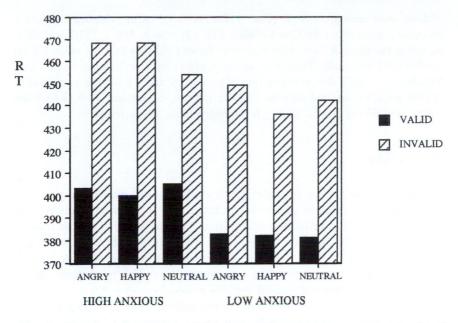

Figure 2. Mean reaction times ini ms (RT) for high and low trait anxious people as a function of cue validity and cue valence in Experiment 1.

$p < .020$, while the predicted Trait Anxiety × Cue Validity × Cue Valence interaction approached significance, *Pillais* $F(2, 31) = 3.08, p < .060$. In order to break down this three-way interaction we examined the data for high and low anxious groups separately.

High trait anxiety. A 2 (Cue Validity) × 3 (Cue Valence) ANOVA revealed the predicted interaction, *Pillais* $F(2, 19) = 8.02, p < .003$. Further analysis revealed that there was no main effect for Cue Valence on the valid trials. However, as expected, there was a significant main effect for Cue Valence on the invalid trials, *Pillais* $F(2, 19) = 6.62, p < .007$. Paired *t*-tests revealed that RTs following angry faces were slower (468 ms) than RTs following neutral, 454 ms: $t(20) = 3.59, p < .001$, but not happy, 468 ms: $t(20) < 1$ faces. Reaction times following happy faces did not differ from RTs following neutral faces, 468 ms vs. 454 ms: $t(20) = 1.69, p < .106$, 2-tailed. Planned comparisons revealed that the cue validity effect with angry faces (mean = 66 ms, confidence interval [CI] = 53.6 to 77.6) was larger than that observed for neutral faces, mean = 49 ms; CI = 38.4 to 59.9: $t(20) = 3.76, p < .001$, but was comparable to the cue validity effect for happy faces, mean = 68 ms; CI = 50.9 to 84.7: $t(20) < 1$. There was also a difference between the cue validity effect with happy faces (68 ms) relative to neutral faces, 49 ms: $t(20) = 2.25, p < .036$, 2-tailed.

Low trait anxiety. A 2 (Cue Validity) × 3 (Cue Valence) ANOVA revealed a main effect for Cue Validity, $F(1, 12) = 96.8$, $MS_e = 737.7$, $p < .001$, such that the mean RT on valid trials was faster (382 ms) than the mean RT on invalid (442 ms) trials. There was no main effect for Cue Valence and no Cue Validity × Cue Valence interaction. The means and CI for the cue validity effects were 61 ms, and 44.9 to 77.4 for neutral, 54 ms and 39.9 to 68.9 for happy, and 66 ms and 52.3 to 79.6 for angry faces, respectively.

Discussion

As expected, there was a large cue validity effect in this experiment such that participants were faster in categorising a target that appeared in a validly cued location relative to an invalidly cued location. The magnitude of the cue validity effect did not differ between the high and low anxiety groups. As we used a target *categorisation* task, this cue validity effect can be attributed to an attentional mechanism, rather than a response preparation mechanism, as the location of the cue was not predictive of the required response. Of more interest, an interaction between the valence of the cue and the level of self-reported trait anxiety of the participant had a bearing on the magnitude of the cue validity effect. Specifically, high trait anxious people took longer to categorise a target when it appeared in an invalidly cued location when the cue had been an emotionally valenced face (angry or happy), relative to when the face had been emotionally neutral. We predicted this pattern for *angry* facial expressions but the enhanced attentional dwell-time for *happy* facial expressions was unexpected. It is worth noting that this general emotionality effect has been sometimes reported in the literature (e.g., with homophones: Russo, Patterson, Roberson, Stevenson, & Upward, 1996) but does not seem to be consistent. For the low trait anxious participants, the valence of the cue made little difference to the speed of response on either the validly or the invalidly cued trials. Although the valence of the cue had no statistically significant effect for the low trait anxious participants, it is worth noting that the magnitude of the cue validity effects did not differ between the anxiety groups for either angry, happy, or neutral face cues (66 ms vs. 66 ms; 68 ms vs. 54 ms; 49 ms vs. 61 ms, respectively: all *t*s < 1.3). Nevertheless, reaction times on invalid trials did not differ across cue types for the low anxious group, while they did increase significantly following angry and happy faces relative to neutral faces for the high anxious group. The real issue here is how best to measure bias, between groups or between within-subject conditions? Our view is that, although the cue validity effects might have been similar for the angry faces between the high and the low trait anxious groups, the proportional increase in cue validity effects between the neutral and the angry faces was different for the low anxious and the high anxious groups (.07 and .26, respectively). This demonstrates that there is a difference in how high trait anxious people respond to different classes of emotional stimuli.

EXPERIMENT 2

The findings of Experiment 1 suggested that an emotionally valenced facial expression produced delayed disengagement in high trait anxious people. Our previous research has found similar results with variations of state anxiety, although usually the pattern has been specific to *angry* facial expressions, and has not been found for *happy* facial expressions. Similar to the current results, a recent study using pictorial stimuli has found that high trait anxious people take longer to disengage attention from the location of emotionally threatening pictures (Yiend & Mathews, in press). The Yiend and Mathews study did not include emotional pictures with a positive valence and therefore it is not known whether similar results would occur with positive and negative stimuli, relative to neutral stimuli. Because we generally found differences in disengaging attention from the location of angry faces and not from happy faces in our previous research (Fox et al., in press), we are inclined to believe that increased dwell-time should be particularly salient with threatening stimuli. However, there is some evidence against this in a recent investigation of three people with chronic unilateral neglect and visual extinction (Vuilleumier & Schwartz, 2001). On trials in which line drawings were presented simultaneously to the left and right visual fields, these patients extinguished schematic faces in the contrale-sional field much less often than shapes. Of more relevance, faces with angry or happy expressions were extinguished much less than faces with a neutral expression (Vuilleumier & Schwartz, 2001). Thus, faces with either a positive or a negative emotional expression did not differ in terms of capturing attention, but both were more effective than neutral faces. Therefore, it might be the case that the brain mechanisms involved in producing enhanced dwell-time on visual stimuli might not differentiate between positive and negative emotional expressions.

Experiment 2 further tested attentional disengagement from the location of emotional facial expressions (angry and happy) relative to neutral facial expressions. The cue-target stimulus onset asynchrony (SOA) was increased from 300 ms to 960 ms, thus rendering this an IOR task. The logic is as follows: if an angry (or happy) face holds attention for a longer period of time than a neutral face, then the magnitude of IOR should be reduced for angry (or happy) face cues over the same time scale. This is because attention will be held for longer in the location of an angry (or happy) cue and thus will not drift back to a central location in time for the application of inhibitory processes. To our knowledge, this is the first modification of the IOR paradigm in which faces with varying emotional expressions are used as cues. One of the problems is choosing an appropriate SOA given that we do not know the precise time scale of disengagement especially concerning possible anxiety-related differences. However, an SOA of 960 is fairly standard in the IOR literature and we also conducted a pilot study with low trait anxious people using neutral and jumbled face cues and found a typical IOR effect of around 19 ms with an SOA of 960 ms. Thus, as a first step we tested for cue valence differences using a standard SOA. We do acknowledge, however, that anxiety-related differences may be difficult to detect until more is known about the time scale of disengagement processes. Thus, on the basis of previous research (e.g., Fox et al., in press; Yiend & Mathews, in press), we tentatively predicted an interaction between Trait Anxiety, Cue Validity, and Cue Valence such that high anxious people will demonstrate a reduced IOR effect to angry faces, relative to neutral faces. Given the results of Experiment 1, we might also expect a reduced IOR effect for happy facial expressions.

Three key changes were made from Experiment 1. First, the SOA was increased from 300 ms to 960 ms. Second, target localisation was used rather than target categorisation. Although this reintroduces some of the problems outlined in Experiment 1 it was considered necessary because previous research has shown that IOR often does not occur with categorisation tasks but is reliable with localisation tasks (Klein & Taylor, 1994). This methodological change, of course, allows for the possibility that response preparation effects may influence the results. However, we would argue that differences in the magnitude of the IOR effect are interesting regardless of whether attentional or response preparation mechanisms is the primary determinant of IOR. The possibility that participants might strategically attend to just one side of the screen and respond to that side if something occurs there, and to the other side if nothing occurs is unlikely, but something that cannot be excluded. Third, the percentage of valid and invalid trials was 50/50 because IOR is eliminated if the proportion of valid trials is higher than 50% (see Klein & Taylor, 1994, for review).

Method

Participants.   These were 48 undergraduate students from the University of Essex campus community. Participants ranged in age from 18 to 32 years with a modal age in the 20s. Those scoring at or above a score of 40 ($n = 25$) on the STAI trait anxiety scale and those scoring at or below 35 ($n = 23$) were classified as high and low trait anxious participants respectively. Each person had normal or corrected-to-normal eyesight and participated in one experimental session as part of an undergraduate laboratory class.

Materials and procedure.   The schematic "neutral", "happy", and "angry" faces from Experiment 1 were used (see Figure 1). The target that participants had to localise was a black circle with a diameter of 0.4 cm. Cue and target stimuli were presented inside two light grey boxes that were 5.3 cm high and 3.0 cm wide and were displayed 2.0 cm to the left and the right of the central fixation point (cross shape). These squares were continuously present on the computer screen. All stimuli were presented on a MacIntosh computer with a 28 cm colour monitor.

The procedure was the same as Experiment 1. The sequence of events within each trial differed from Experiment 1 as follows. A fixation point (X) was presented at the centre of the screen for 800 ms. A face cue was then presented in one of the peripheral boxes for 300 ms. The cue was subsequently blanked out and 200 ms later the central cross was darkened for a further 300 ms. The initial fixation display was then presented for 160 ms and then the target was presented in the lower half of either the left or the right box until the participant responded (or until 2000 ms elasped). This gave a cue-target onset asynchrony (SOA) of 960 ms. There was an intertrial interval of 1000 ms. See Figure 3 for a graphic example of a single trial.

Each participant completed 16 practice trials, followed by 360 experimental trials, divided into five blocks of 72. Of the experimental trials, 50% (180) were valid (i.e., the target appeared in the same spatial location as the cue), and 50% (180) were invalid (i.e., the target appeared in the opposite spatial location to the cue). Neutral, happy and angry face cues appeared 60 times each on valid trials and 60 times each on invalid trials. The probability of any particular cue appearing in the left- and right-handside boxes was equal. Participants were told that the position of the face did not predict the location of the target and therefore they should ignore the face and keep their eyes focused on the centre of the screen and respond as quickly and as accurately as possible.

Design.   A 2 (Anxiety: high and low trait anxiety) × 2 (Cue Validity: valid and invalid) × 3 (Cue Valence: neutral, happy, and angry) ANOVA factorial design was used. Trait anxiety was a between-subjects factor while Cue Validity and Cue Valence were within-subjects factors. The main prediction was a Trait Anxiety × Cue Validity × Cue Valence interaction such that IOR effects (i.e., slower RTs on valid relative to invalid trials) should be *reduced* on angry face trials compared to neutral face trials. We might also expect a reduced IOR effect on happy relative to neutral face trials given the results of Experiment 1. This reduced IOR effect on angry (and happy) face trials was expected to be particularly strong for high trait anxious participants.

Results

As shown in Table 1, the high trait anxious group scored significantly higher on the measure of state-anxiety compared to the low trait anxious group.

Incorrect responses (< 1% of trials) and RT latencies of below 150 ms or above 1200 ms were eliminated from the RT data. The mean correct RT data are shown in Figure 4. These data were subjected to a 2 (Trait Anxiety: high and low

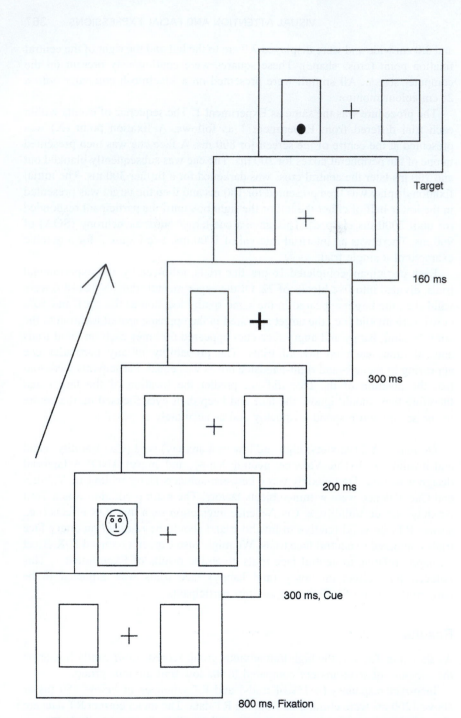

Figure 3. Diagram of a valid trial in the IOR paradigm used in Experiment 2 and 3.

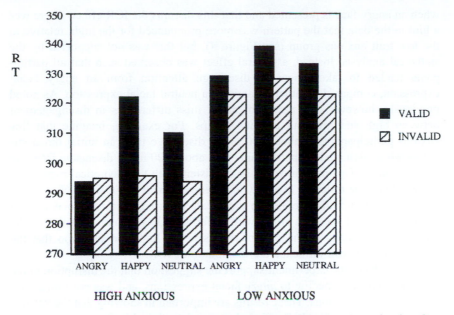

Figure 4.   Mean reaction times in ms (RT) for high and low trait anxious people as a function of cue validity and cue valence in Experiment 2.

trait-anxiety) × 2 (Cue Validity: valid and invalid) × 3 (Cue Valence: neutral, happy, angry) ANOVA with participants as a random factor. There were main effects for Trait Anxiety, $F(1, 46) = 4.35$, $MS_e = 12,536.7$, $p < .042$, and for Cue Validity, $F(1, 46) = 51.9$, $MS_e = 179.6$, $p < .001$. There was a significant Cue Validity × Cue Valence interaction, *Pillais* $F(2, 45) = 3.94$, $p < .027$, while the Trait Anxiety × Cue Validity × Cue Valence interaction did not reach significance, *Pillais* $F(2, 45) = 1.28$, $p < .288$.

Further analysis for all participants (high and low trait anxious combined) revealed that a significant IOR effect occurred for both Happy, mean $= -19$ ms; CI $= -10.2$ to -27.2: $t(47) = 4.43$, $p < .001$, and Neutral, mean $= -14$ ms; CI $= -9.6$ to -17.7: $t(47) = 6.76$, $p < .001$, but not for Angry, mean $= -2$ ms; CI $= -5.2$ to 9.5: $t(47) < 1$ face cues. Likewise, the IOR effects with Happy and Neutral face cues did not differ from each other $t(47) = 1.29$, while both Happy, $t(47) = 2.32$, $p < .025$, and Neutral, $t(47) = 2.83$, $p < .007$ face cues produced a greater magnitude of IOR than Angry face cues.

Discussion

As predicted, the magnitude of IOR was significantly less when angry facial expressions were used as cues, relative to either happy or neutral facial expressions. This supports our assumption that attentional dwell-time increases when an angry face is presented and that this disrupts the IOR effect. There was a hint in the data that the pattern was more pronounced for the high, relative to the low trait anxious group (see Figure 4), but this was not supported by the statistical analysis. Instead, a general effect was observed such that all participants tended to take longer to disengage attention from an angry facial expression, compared to either a happy or a neutral facial expression. As noted previously, however, this paradigm might miss differences in disengagement between high and low trait anxious groups. For example, imagine that low anxious participants take about 300 ms to disengage from an initial threat stimulus while high anxious participants take about 600 ms to disengage from the same stimulus. This pattern would be consistent with the theoretical hypothesis but would not be reflected in any IOR differences with an SOA of 960 ms. Our ongoing research will examine the time scale of disengagement processes and the magnitude of the IOR effect with different SOAs in more detail. For the moment, the novelty of the current results is the first demonstration that the valence of a cue can influence the magnitude of IOR.

The results of the experiment support the suggestion that the disruption to the IOR mechanism is specific to *angry* facial expressions, and was not found with happy facial expressions. These results are important in showing that the valence of a cue can disrupt the IOR effect. It is worth noting that these results with a sample of nonbrain damaged young adults are conceptually similar to the finding that people with right parietal damage do not extinguish emotional faces (angry or happy) as efficiently as neutral faces (Veuilleumier & Schwartz, 2001). As a general point, therefore, it seems that the valence or meaning of a stimulus can disrupt IOR. We discuss this further in the General Discussion.

EXPERIMENT 3

Experiment 2 supported the hypothesis that angry facial expressions might disrupt the IOR effect. However, the results of Experiment 2 showed that any differences between high and low trait anxious people in terms of how disruptive the angry facial expression was to the IOR effect did not reach statistical significance. One possibility is that all individuals are equally affected in paradigms of this type by a potentially threatening stimulus. It makes adaptive sense not to inhibit returning attention to the location of potential threat. Alternatively, there may have been differences that were not detected by this task because the SOA was not appropriate. Finally, it is also possible that the high trait anxious participants in our study did not differ from low anxious people on the IOR task because they did not have elevated levels of state anxiety. Previous research has shown that attentional effects are often determined by a complex interaction between levels of trait and state anxiety (e.g., MacLeod & Mathews, 1988; Mogg et al., 1994). Moreover, our previous research on attentional disengagement found that state anxiety was a stronger determinant of delayed disengagement than trait anxiety (Fox et al., in press). Therefore, we hypothe-sised that we might find differences in attentional disengagement between high and low trait anxious participants if levels of state anxiety were elevated above baseline. To this aim, we introduced a simple mood induction procedure in Experiment 3 in an attempt to elevate state anxiety above baseline levels. Once again, the IOR paradigm was presented to high and low trait anxious partici-pants, but this time following a task requiring participants to rate distressing photographs for threat value. Previous research in our laboratory has shown that this procedure is often successful in increasing the level of self-reported state anxiety. As before, we predict a Trait Anxiety × Cue Validity × Cue Valence interaction such that high trait anxious people will show reduced IOR for angry face cues, relative to neutral face cues. In this experiment we included the angry and neutral facial expressions from the previous experiments as well as a jumbled face. The jumbled face consisted of the features of the angry face (see Figure 1) and was included because pilot work with low trait anxious partici-pants has shown that we get standard IOR effects with jumbled face stimuli. Moreover, if we get a different pattern of results with the normal angry and the jumbled angry face we can rule out the possibility that some low-level visual feature of the face was producing the results, rather than the emotional expression of the face (see Fox et al., 2000, for further discussion). In contrast, if we find a similar pattern of results with the normal and the jumbled angry faces we can conclude that a particular feature of the face is producing the results rather than the holistic facial expression.

Method

Participants.   These were 80 undergraduate students from the University of Essex or the University of Padua campus communities. Participants ranged in age from 18 to 40 years with a modal age in the 20s. Those scoring at or above a score of 40 ($n = 43$) on the STAI trait anxiety scale and those scoring at or below 35 ($n = 37$) were classified as high and low trait anxious participants respectively. Each person had normal or corrected-to-normal eyesight and participated in one experimental session lasting about 45 minutes for which they received payment of £4.00, or course credits.

Materials and procedure.   The schematic "angry" and "neutral" faces from Experiment 1 were used in addition to a jumbled face (see Figure 1). The target, which participants had to localise was a white circle with a diameter of 0.3 cm. Cue and target stimuli were presented inside two dark grey boxes that were 5.3 cm high and 3.0 cm wide, and were displayed 2.0 cm to the left and the right of the central fixation point (cross shape). These boxes were continuously present on the computer screen. All stimuli were presented on a Pentium P5/120 PC with a 28 cm colour monitor and ATI Mach64 graphics card. All stimulus presentation and data collection was controlled by MEL software Version 2 (Schneider, 1988).

Early in the academic year, participants completed the STAI: trait and state (baseline) anxiety scales in a group testing session. On arrival at the laboratory, each participant was shown 10 colour photographs taken from magazine articles showing scenes from war zones (e.g., victims of war, mutilated bodies, etc.). They were told this was part of a separate study and asked to rate each photograph on a 7-point scale from "pleasant" to "extremely threatening". Participants did not spend more than about 2 minutes on any of the photographs. The aim of this simple mood induction procedure was to attempt to elevate state anxiety levels above baseline. Each participant then completed the STAI state anxiety scale, which gave a measure of state anxiety at test. On completion of the state anxiety questionnaire, participants were asked to move to a computer in the same room for the reaction time experiment, where they were seated about 50 cm from the computer monitor. The task was identical to Experiment 2 except that a jumbled face was presented instead of the happy face.

Design.   A 2 (Trait Anxiety: high and low trait anxiety) × 2 (Cue Validity: valid and invalid) × 3 (Cue Valence: neutral, angry, and jumbled) ANOVA factorial design was used. Trait anxiety was a between-subjects factor while Cue Validity and Cue Valence were within-subjects factors. The main prediction was a Trait Anxiety × Cue Validity × Cue Valence interaction such that IOR effects (i.e., slower RTs on valid relative to invalid trials) were expected to be *reduced* on angry face trials compared to either neutral or jumbled face trials. This reduced IOR effect on angry face trials was expected to be particularly strong for high trait anxious participants.

Results

As shown in Table 1, the high trait anxious group scored significantly higher on measures of state anxiety compared to the low trait anxious group. A 2 (Anxiety: high and low trait anxiety) × 2 (Time of Testing: state anxiety at baseline and test) ANOVA revealed main effects for Trait Anxiety group, $F(1, 78) = 63.8$, $MS_e = 72.9$, $p < .001$, and for Time of Testing, $F(1, 78) = 21.4$, $MS_e = 36.6$, $p < .001$. There was also a Trait Anxiety × Time of Testing interaction, $F(1, 78) = 15.1$, $MS_e = 36.6$, $p < .001$. Further analysis showed that state anxiety increased from baseline to test for the high trait anxious group, $t(42) = 5.02$, $p < .001$, but not for the low trait anxious group, $t(36) < 1$.

Incorrect responses (< 1% of trials) and RT latencies of below 150 ms or above 1200 ms were eliminated from the data. The mean correct RT data are shown in Figure 5. These data were subjected to a 2 (Trait Anxiety: high and low trait-anxiety) × 2 (Cue Validity: valid and invalid) × 3 (Cue Valence: neutral, happy, angry) ANOVA with participants as a random factor. There was a main

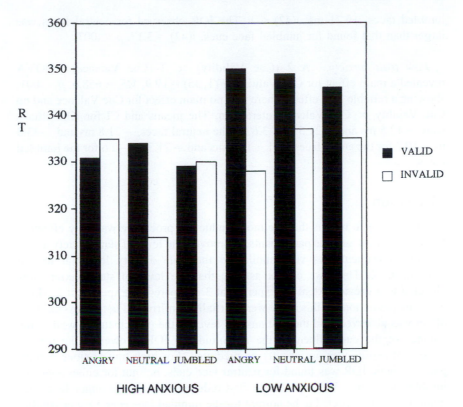

Figure 5. Mean reaction times in ms (RT) for high and low trait anxious people as a function of cue validity and cue valence in Experiment 3.

effect for Cue Validity, $F(1, 78) = 16.8$, $MS_e = 739.3$, $p < .001$, showing an IOR effect. Of greater theoretical importance, however, the predicted Trait Anxiety × Cue Validity × Cue Valence interaction was significant, $F(2, 156) = 6.78$, $p < .002$. In order to break down this three-way interaction we examined the data for high and low anxious groups separately.

High trait anxiety. A 2 (Cue Validity) × 3 (Cue Valence) ANOVA revealed the predicted interaction, $F(2, 84) = 8.13$, $p < .001$. Further analysis revealed that the IOR effect was significant for neutral face cues, mean = −19 ms; CI = −28.1 to −10.1: $t(42) = 4.3$, $p < .001$, but not for either angry, mean = +3.4 ms; CI = −8.1 to 14.9: $t(42) < 1$, or jumbled (mean = −0.71; CI = −8.9 to 10.3: $t(42) < 1$ face cues. Planned comparisons revealed that the IOR effect with angry faces (+3.3 ms) was smaller than that observed for neutral faces, −19 ms: $t(42) = 3.6$, $p < .001$, but was comparable to that observed for jumbled faces, +0.71 ms: $t(42) < 1$. The IOR observed for neutral faces was larger than that found for jumbled face cues, $t(42) = 3.17$, $p < .003$.

Low trait anxiety. A 2 (Cue Validity) × 3 (Cue Valence) ANOVA revealed a main effect for Cue Validity, $F(1, 36) = 19.9$, $MS_e = 658.6$, $p < .001$, showing a reliable IOR effect. There was no main effect for Cue Valence and no Cue Validity × Cue Valence interaction. The means and CI for IOR effects were -12.5 ms and -21.5 to -3.6 for the neutral faces, -21.8 ms and -33.3 to -10.2 for the angry faces, and -11.9 ms and -21.3 to -2.6 for the jumbled faces.

Discussion

The first point to note is that the mood induction procedure was only effective for the high trait anxious participants. Moreover, the level of state anxiety at test in this experiment was very similar to the state anxiety levels at test in Experiment 2. Thus, we cannot assume that the level of state anxiety was elevated to a greater extent in Experiment 3 compared to Experiment 2. However, the predictions of this study were partially confirmed. First, an overall IOR effect was observed, and the trait anxiety level of the participant, as well as the valence of the cue influenced the magnitude of IOR. However, the precise pattern of results was not exactly as predicted. For high trait anxious participants, reliable IOR was found for neutral face cues, but not for either angry *or* jumbled face cues. We expected to find reduced IOR for the angry face cues while IOR was expected to be normal for the jumbled face cues. One possibility is that because the jumbled face comprised the jumbled features of an *angry* face, perhaps one or more of the features (e.g., eyebrows) of the angry face was a fundamental threat signal which led subsequently to delayed disengagement. There is some evidence for this speculation from research showing that downward turned eyebrows, as used here, are important determinants of the threat value of schematic faces (Aronoff, Woike, & Hyman, 1992; Lundqvist, Esteves, & Öhman, 1999). Thus, it might have been the case that the high trait anxious people delayed disengaging from the eyebrow stimuli even when they were embedded in a jumbled face. In a partial attempt to confirm this, we asked 12 adults from the campus community to rate the angry, neutral, and jumbled angry faces on a 1–7 scale (1 = very positive, 7 = very threatening). The stimuli were presented on pages in a random order and were embedded among "happy" and jumbled "happy" and "neutral" schematic face stimuli. The results showed a significant difference in the threat ratings for the stimuli used in this experiment (angry, neutral, jumbled angry), $F(2, 22) = 48.6$, $MS_e = 0.76$, $p < .001$. Follow-up t-tests (2-tailed) revealed that the "angry" face was rated as more threatening (mean = 6.4) than the "neutral" face, mean = 3.1; $t(11) = 9.4$, $p < .001$, but did not differ significantly from the jumbled angry face, mean = 5.7; $t(11) = 2.0$,

$p < .07$). The "jumbled angry" face was rated as significantly more threatening than the neutral "face", 5.7 vs. 3.1; $t(11) = 7.7$, $p < .001$. Thus, the rating data give some weight to the notion that the jumbled face may have been perceived as a threatening stimulus in this experiment, and that this is why the magnitude of IOR to these stimuli was not significant for high trait anxious individuals. An alternative possibility is that it was not the threat value of the jumbled face that was important, but rather, its ambiguity. As can be seen in Figure 1, the jumbled cue is face-like but it's expression is ambiguous. Thus, it may have been the emotional ambiguity of the jumbled face that was important in driving the results than the threat value *per se*. It is therefore possible that the reduced IOR effect with jumbled faces reflects a more general emotionality effect, rather than a threat-specific effect.

The results for the low trait anxious participants were as expected. This group showed a strong IOR effect and this did not differ across the three types of cue (angry, neutral, and jumbled). Thus, the results of this experiment provide some support for the notion that high trait anxious participants, under conditions of elevated state anxiety, take longer to disengage from threat-related and emotionally ambiguous facial stimuli. This was reflected in a reduced IOR effect following angry (and jumbled angry) face cues relative to neutral face cues.

GENERAL DISCUSSION

Although it is well established that visual attention is automatically captured by the sudden onset of a new perceptual object (Yantis, 1996), the novelty of the present study is that we manipulated the *valence* of a briefly presented object. Following Fox et al. (in press), this was achieved by using schematic faces with angry, neutral or happy expressions as the *cue* in Posner's (1980) cueing paradigm. The logic was as follows: If angry faces are particularly effective in holding visual attention (i.e., increasing dwell-time), then (i) response times should *increase* on invalid trials following threat cues when the SOA is short, and (ii) when the SOA is long, the magnitude of the IOR effect should be *reduced* on trials with threat-related cues. The hypothesis that angry facial expressions would lead to enhanced dwell-time (delayed disengagement), especially in high trait-anxious individuals, was partially supported in these studies.

First, in Experiment 1 with a short SOA, we did find that the valence of the cue affected the cue validity effect only for high trait anxious individuals. However, the pattern of results was not exactly as predicted. The results showed that the high trait anxious people took longer to disengage from angry *and* happy facial expressions, relative to neutral expressions as reflected by increased response times on invalid trials. Response times on invalid trials were equivalent across the different cue types for the low trait anxious participants. Thus, the presence of an emotionally valenced face (positive or negative) resulted in delayed disengagement in high, but not in low, trait anxious people.

In Experiment 2, the SOA was increased to assess whether the magnitude of IOR would be reduced with angry face cues, relative to happy or neutral face cues in high trait anxious people. However, the results did not confirm an anxiety-linked disruption of the IOR effect with angry facial expressions as cues. Instead, it was found that *all* participants showed a reduced IOR effect with angry facial expressions as cues, relative to either happy or neutral facial expressions. The results of this experiment support the notion that there is something special about *angry* faces, and that, contrary to the findings of Experiment 1, attentive resources are not necessarily disrupted by faces expressing positive as well as threatening emotions. It seems likely that evolution would have favoured the capacity to efficiently process and respond to threat signals (e.g., an angry face) in the visual environment. In line with this, Öhman and Soares (1993) found that fear-relevant stimuli, such as snakes and angry faces, were special in that they were processed at a pre-attentive level with no apparent need for conscious representation before a phobic response could be elicited. This result is also consistent with evidence that negative social information is more "attention grabbing" than positive social information (Pratto & John, 1991).

In Experiment 3, an interaction was found between IOR and trait anxiety such that high trait anxious people showed reduced IOR to angry and jumbled face cues, relative to neutral face cues. Low trait anxious people showed an equivalent amount of IOR across the three cue types. In retrospect, we realised that constructing the jumbled face from the features of an angry face was unwise. It is possible that a key feature of the angry face, such as the down-turned eyebrows, might have led to the disruption of the IOR effect. For example, it has been found that these features are especially important in determining the threat value of a face (Lundqvist et al., 1999). A *post-hoc* rating of the stimuli used in Experiment 3 supported this notion in showing that the jumbled face was rated as more threatening than the neutral face, and the rating was almost as high as the "angry" face. However, as noted previously the emotional ambiguity of the face might have been confusing and the ambiguity might be more important that the threat value of the jumbled face in affecting IOR. Thus, the results of this experiment support the general hypothesis that the presence of threat or ambiguous cues can disrupt the IOR effect in people with high levels of trait anxiety. We argue that this result provides converging evidence for the hypothesis that threatening stimuli lead to delayed disengagement of visual attention in anxious people (Fox et al., in press; Yiend & Mathews, in press). Moreover, the results suggest that emotionally ambiguous stimuli might also delay disengagement processes in high trait anxious people.

These results add tentatively to the growing evidence that people (especially when they are anxious) take longer to disengage from threat-related stimuli such as angry facial expressions (Fox et al., in press) and threatening pictures (Yiend & Mathews, in press). These results are similar to our earlier findings with angry faces, although in that study (Fox et al., in press) we found that the difficulty in disengaging from threatening facial expressions was related to levels of state anxiety and not so strongly to levels of trait anxiety. The question of whether trait or state anxiety is the main determinant of attentional biases towards threat is complex. Some studies find that trait anxiety is a stronger predictor, some that state anxiety is a stronger predictor, and some that the appearance of attentional bias only occurs in high trait anxious individuals when they are experiencing an elevation in state anxiety (e.g., MacLeod & Mathews, 1988; Mogg et al., 1994). For example, MacLeod and Mathews (1988) found that high trait anxious people only showed evidence for attentional bias toward threat words when they were tested prior to end of year examinations and their state anxiety levels were elevated. Even though the state anxiety levels of the low trait anxious participants was also elevated this group did not show any bias towards threat. Thus, an interaction between trait and state anxiety seems important. In our future research, we intend to test participants in both low and high stress periods to investigate the relations between state and trait anxiety and performance on IOR tasks more directly.

It is worth noting at this point that the results observed in our IOR experiments (Experiments 2 and 3) appear to support an attentional account of IOR and not a motor account. As noted in the introduction, the attentional account (e.g., Posner & Cohen, 1984) explains IOR as a reflection of attention being inhibited from returning to a previously attended location. However, Klein and Taylor (1994) have proposed a motor account of IOR which suggests that IOR is a bias against responding to an event that occurs in a location to which a response has previously been prepared. The finding, for example, that IOR only occurs with central cues (e.g., an arrow pointing left or right) if participants were instructed to prepare an eye movement to the cued location supports an non-attentional account of IOR (Rafal, Calabresi, Brennan, & Sciolto, 1989). If IOR is an attentional effect, then it should not matter how attention was allocated to a location. More recent research, however, has supported an attentional account in showing that IOR occurs regardless of whether the response was location or identity-based (Pratt, Kingstone, & Khoe, 1997). For example, Pratt et al. (1997) found IOR even when the spatial mapping between the cue stimulus and the response was orthogonal. This result is inconsistent with a motor account of IOR. Although space does not permit a detailed overview of attentional and motor-based theories of IOR here, we note that the current results would seem to support an attentional account. Even though our paradigm had a strong spatial component (participants responded to the *location* of a target), the fact that the *valence* of the cue influenced the magnitude of IOR suggests that attentional factors are important. Presumably participants prepared a motor response on every trial, but it was only when the cue was threat-related that the IOR was disrupted. In summary, the present results demonstrate for the first time that the valence of a cue can influence the magnitude of the IOR effect. Second, we have shown that individuals with high levels of self-reported trait anxiety are especially sensitive to the valence of a cue in these attentional paradigms. Taken together, these results provide converging evidence that high levels of trait (and state) anxiety may increase attentional dwell-time and disengagement of attention from threat-related stimuli. Our current research is concerned with investigating the time course of this phenomenon.

Manuscript received 1 November 2000
Revised manuscript received 4 May 2001

REFERENCES

Armony, J., & LeDoux, J.E. (2000). How danger is encoded: Toward a systems, cellular, and computational understanding of cognitive-emotional interactions in fear. In M.S. Gazzaniga (Ed.), *The new cognitive neurosciences* (2nd ed., pp. 1067–1079). Cambridge, MA: MIT Press.

Aronoff, J., Woike, B.A., & Hyman, L.M. (1992). Which are the stimuli in facial displays of anger and happiness? Configurational bases of emotion recognition. *Journal of Personality and Social Psychology, 62*, 1050–1066.

Bradley, B., Mogg, K., Falla, S.J., & Hamilton, L.R. (1998). Attentional bias for threatening facial expressions in anxiety: Manipulation of stimulus duration. *Cognition and Emotion, 12*, 737–753.

Eysenck, M.W. (1992). *Anxiety: The cognitive perspective*. Hove, UK: Psychology Press.

Eysenck, M.W. (1997). *Anxiety and cognition: A unified theory*. Hove, UK: Psychology Press.

Fox, E. (1993). Allocation of visual attention and anxiety. *Cognition and Emotion, 7*, 207–215.

Fox, E. (in press). Processing emotional facial expressions: The role of anxiety and awareness. *Cognitive, affective and behavioral Neuroscience.*

Fox, E., Lester, V., Russo, R., Bowles, R.J., Pichler, A., & Dutton, K. (2000). Facial expressions of emotion: Are angry faces detected more efficiently? *Cognition and Emotion, 14*, 61–92.

Fox, E., Russo, R., Bowles, R., & Dutton, K. (2001). Do threatening stimuli draw or hold attention in subclinical anxiety? *Journal of Experimental Psychology: General, 130*, 681–700.

Klein, R.M., & Taylor, T.L. (1994). Categories of cognition inhibition with reference to attention. In D. Dagenbach & T.H. Carr (Eds.), *Inhibitory processes in attention, memory, and language.* (pp. 113–150). San Diego, CA: Academic Press.

LeDoux, J. (1996). *The emotional brain*. New York: Simon & Schuster.

Lundqvist, D., Esteves, F., & Öhman, A. (1999). The face of wrath: Critical features for conveying facial threat. *Cognition and Emotion, 13*, 691–711.

Macleod, C., & Mathews, A. (1988). Anxiety and the allocation of attention to threat. *Quarterly Journal of Experimental Psychology, 40A*, 653–670.

MacLeod, C., Mathews, A., & Tata, P. (1986). Attentional bias in emotional disorders. *Journal of Abnormal Psychology, 95*, 15–20.

Mathews, A.M., & MacLeod, C. (1994). Cognitive approaches to emotion and emotional disorders. *Annual Review of Psychology, 45*, 25–50.

Mogg, K., Bradley, B., & Hallowel, N. (1994). Attentional bias to threat: Roles of trait anxiety, stressful events, and awareness. *Quarterly Journal of Experimental Psychology, 47A*, 841–864.

Navon, D., & Margalit, B. (1983). Allocation of attention according to informativeness in visual recognition. *Quarterly Journal of Experimental Psychology, 35A*, 497–512.

Öhman, A. (1993). Fear and anxiety as emotional phenomenon: Clinical phenomenology, evolutionary perspectives, and information-processing mechanisms. In M. Lewis & J.M. Haviland (Eds.), *Handbook of Emotions* (pp. 511–536). New York: Guilford Press.

Öhman, A., & Soares, J.F. (1993). On the automatic nature of phobic fear: Conditioned electrodermal responses to masked fear-relevant stimuli. *Journal of Abnormal Psychology, 102,* 121–132.

Posner, M.I. (1980). Orienting of attention. *Quarterly Journal of Experimental Psychology, 32A,* 3–25.

Posner, M.I., & Cohen, Y. (1984). Components of visual orienting. In H. Bouma & D. Bowhuis (Eds.), *Attention and performance X* (pp. 531–556). Hove, UK: Lawrence Erlbaum Associates Ltd.

Pratt, J., Kingstone, A., & Khoe, W. (1997). Inhibition of return in location- and identity-based choice decision tasks. *Perception and Psychophysics, 59,* 964–971.

Pratto, F., & John, O.P. (1991). Automatic vigilance: The attention grabbing power of negative social information. *Journal of Personality and Social Psychology, 61,* 380–391.

Rafal, R.D., Calabresi, P.A., Brennan, C.W., & Sciolto, T.K. (1989). Saccade preparation inhibits reorienting to recently attended locations. *Journal of Experimental Psychology: Human Perception and Performance, 15,* 673–685.

Russo, R., Patterson, N., Roberson, D., Stevenson, N., & Upward, J. (1996). Emotional value of information and its relevance in the interpretation of homophones in anxiety. *Cognition and Emotion, 10,* 213–220.

Schneider (1988). Micro Experimental Laboratory: An integrated system for IBM-PC compatibles. *Behavior Research Methods, Instruments, and Computers, 20,* 206–217.

Spielberger, C.D., Gorsuch, R.L., Lushene, R., Vagg, P.R., & Jacobs, G.A. (1983). *Manual for the State-Trait Anxiety Inventory.* Palo Alto, CA: Consulting Psychologists Press.

Vuilleumier, P., & Schwartz, S. (2001). Spatial attention is affected by emotional expression of faces: a study of visual neglect and extinction. *Neurology, 56,* 153–158.

Williams, J.M.G., Watts, F.N., MacLeod, C., & Mathews, A. (1988). *Cognitive psychology and emotional disorders.* Chichester, UK: Wiley.

Williams, J.M.G., Watts, F.N., MacLeod, C., & Mathews, A. (1997). *Cognitive psychology and emotional disorders* (2nd ed.) Chichester, UK: Wiley.

Yantis, S. (1996). Attentional Capture in Vision. In A.F. Kramer, M.G.H. Coles., & G.D. Logan (Eds.), *Converging operations in the study of visual selective attention.* Washington, DC: American Psychological Association.

Yiend, J., & Mathews, A.M. (2001). Anxiety and attention to threatening pictures. *Quarterly Journal of Experimental Psychology, 54A,* 665–681.

COGNITION AND EMOTION, 2002, *16* (3), 381–402

Implicit memory bias in depression

Philip C. Watkins

Eastern Washington University, WA, USA

In this review I describe research conducted in my laboratory concerning implicit mood-congruent memory (MCM) bias in clinical depression. MCM is the tendency for depressed individuals to retrieve more unpleasant information from memory than nondepressed controls, and may be an important maintenance mechanism in depression. MCM has been studied frequently with explicit memory tests, but relatively few studies have investigated MCM using implicit memory tests. I describe several implicit memory studies which show that: (a) an implicit MCM bias does not appear to exist when perceptually driven tests are used; (b) implicit memory bias can be found when conceptually driven tests are used, but (c) not all conceptually driven tests show implicit MCM bias. I conclude that conceptual processing is necessary, but is not sufficient for demonstrating implicit memory bias in depression. Future studies should investigate specific components of conceptual elaboration that support implicit memory bias in depression.

Mood-congruent memory (MCM) refers to the tendency for individuals to recall information that is conceptually congruent with their mood. Interest in mood-congruent processes arose out of the work of Gordon Bower and his concern with mood-state dependent memory (e.g., Bower, 1981). Although mood-state dependent memory and MCM are related, in mood-state dependent memory the content of the material learned is not important, only the transfer of learning due to the consistency of mood at study and test. In MCM experiments, mood states at study and test may not be manipulated, but the emotional valence of the information is important. For example, MCM in depression refers to the tendency for depressed individuals to recall more negative or unpleasant material, relative to nondepressed controls.

Correspondence should be addressed to Philip C. Watkins, Department of Psychology, Eastern Washington University, 151 Martin Hall, Cheney, WA, 99004, USA; philip.watkins@mail.ewu.edu

Although many have contributed to the ongoing progress of the research programme outlined in this paper, I would particularly like to thank Corby Martin, Stephanie Muller, Dean Grimm, and Anthony Whitney; four students who have been essential to my laboratory work in the last nine years. I would also like to thank Leonard Stern; his advice and expertise have been invaluable to this research.

 DOI:10.1080/0269993014300536

MCM appears to be a reliable phenomenon in depression. Studies conducted with pleasant and unpleasant words, and with autobiographical recollection have shown that depressives tend to show a more negativistic memory bias than controls (for a review, see Blaney, 1986). In explicit memory, this bias is often revealed by nondepressed participants recalling more positive information than depressives, rather than depressed individuals actually retrieving more negative information than controls. In this review I define MCM bias in depression as a more negative memory bias, which may also mean a lack of a positive memory bias relative to controls.

MCM appears to be so robust, some have proposed that it might be an important maintenance mechanism in depression. For example, Teasdale (1983) has observed that if unpleasant memories are more accessible to depressed persons, remembering these events might help maintain their depressed mood. In addition, Teasdale has suggested that this memory bias might contribute to the depressed individual's failure to engage in effective mood-repair activities. The findings related to MCM indicate that for depressives, unpleasant experiences should be more accessible for recollection. The greater accessibility of these memories might result in lowered expectancy for the success of certain coping activities, thus decreasing the likelihood that the depressed person will initiate mood-repair behaviours. For example, if a depressed person were invited to a social event, MCM would imply that unpleasant memories related to the event would be more accessible for recall. The retrieval of these experiences would likely lead to the depressed person anticipating that the social event would not help their mood state, and the event would probably be avoided. Thus, MCM might maintain the depressed mood state through several avenues.

Although MCM bias appears to be robust in depression, the vast majority of studies investigating MCM have used explicit memory tests. In explicit memory tests the instructions "make explicit reference to, and require conscious recollection of, a specific learning experience" (Schacter, 1987, p. 501). The way memory impacts our lives may not always be in an explicit fashion. Consider that many of the tasks of daily routine require memory but do not involve conscious or intentional recollection. For example, walking, driving a car, tying one's shoes, and buttoning one's shirt all require memory, but most do not attempt to recollect the events in which these activities were learned. In fact, as Roediger (1990) has pointed out, if we did attempt to engage in many of these activities by explicitly recollecting the learning experience, it would interfere with the performance of these tasks.

The daily activities that appear to be affected by memory in this way include more complicated behaviours such as social interactions. Clearly, while constructing sentences in conversation we do not attempt to remember our learning experiences of the meanings of the words we choose. Other complex social behaviours appear to be affected by implicit memory as well. Srull and Wyer (1979) showed that when participants were shown words with a hostile connotation, later in an unrelated task participants tended to rate people as more hostile. Srull and Wyer did not ask their participants to attempt to retrieve the words that they saw earlier in making their judgements, but clearly the exposure to the hostile words showed an impact on their social decisions. Similarly, Smith and Branscombe (1988) found that exposing participants to various trait words later affected their trait judgements of somewhat ambiguous descriptions of behaviour. Thus, explicit memory tests probably do not capture how memory affects much of our everyday experience. As Mason and Graf have stated, "we now know, explicit memory is only a small part—the conscious tip of the iceberg—of how memory for recent events influences us in our daily activities" (1993, p. 8).

In the past 20 years, cognitive psychology has taken great interest in implicit or indirect memory tests. Implicit memory has been defined as "memory for information that was acquired during a specific episode and that is expressed on tests in which subjects are not required, and are frequently unable, to deliberately or consciously recollect the previously studied information" (Schacter, 1990, p. 338). With implicit memory tests no reference is made to the learning experience or the use of memory. Thus, retrieval on these tests may be viewed as unintentional (Richardson-Klavehn, Lee, Joubran, & Bjork, 1994). An example of one of the most commonly used implicit memory tests is word stem completion. After studying words a participant is provided with letter stems (e.g., fea____), and is asked to complete them with the first word that comes to mind. Letter stems are typically provided from words that the participant has studied (referred to as the studied or primed words), and from a set of words they have not studied (the unstudied or unprimed set). Participants reliably producing more words from the studied word set than from the unstudied set indicates evidence of implicit memory.

If MCM is an important cognitive maintenance mechanism in depression, it could be argued that the way this bias impacts the behaviour and experience of depressed individuals is more through implicit or unintentional memory than through explicit processes. To return to my earlier example, when depressed individuals are invited to a social event such as a party, it seems unlikely that they would intentionally attempt to recall past experiences with parties. It is more likely that memories of unpleasant party experiences decrease outcome expectancy through implicit retrieval. A past party episode may come to mind, but it seems unlikely that the depressed person would consciously attempt to retrieve such experiences.

It could also be argued that many of the well documented negative thinking biases in depression (usually demonstrated through self-report questionnaires) are supported through cognitive mechanisms such as implicit MCM bias. For example, a cognitive distortion, such as overgeneralisation, could be seen as the result of a depressed person tending to retrieve more unpleasant events and thus making inaccurate negative generalisations about their life. Similarly, the tendency for depressives to dwell on more negative than positive aspects of an experience (referred to by cognitive therapists as the *mental filter*), could be the result of a negative implicit memory bias regarding the event. For example, even though a depressed individual has had many positive interactions at a social event, they may report that they "didn't have any fun" at the occasion because they are dwelling on the one negative interaction that took place. It could be that the reason they are dwelling on this event is that it more easily comes to mind through implicit retrieval. In fact, to anticipate a bit, we have found that a conceptually driven implicit memory bias tends to correlate more with cognitive symptoms of depression than with mood or physical symptoms (Novo & Watkins, 2000). The preceding argument assumes that an implicit memory bias exists in depression. Thus, it is important to establish the existence of an implicit MCM bias, and the conditions in which it is most likely to occur. In brief, these are the issues I attempt to speak to in this review.

I believe that investigations of implicit memory bias in depression may provide important clues to the cognitive mechanisms that maintain depression. In this paper, I describe the various studies conducted in my laboratory that have investigated implicit MCM in depression. In these studies, all of the depressed group participants met DSM criteria for either major depressive disorder or dysthymic disorder. Nondepressed controls had Beck Depression Inventory scores under 6 and did not meet DSM criteria for any mood disorder. I discuss these studies in chronological order, beginning with our study using the perceptually driven implicit test of word stem completion (Watkins, Mathews, Williamson, & Fuller, 1992), in which we failed to demonstrate an implicit MCM bias, despite finding a bias in our explicit memory task. I then describe our initial test of MCM in a conceptually driven implicit memory test (Watkins, Vache, Verney, Muller, & Mathews, 1996), where we did find an implicit memory bias. In our third study we manipulated perceptually driven and conceptually driven processes in implicit memory (Watkins, Martin, & Stern, 2000b). Here we again failed to find any implicit memory bias in our perceptually driven tests, but did demonstrate implicit MCM in one of our two conceptually driven tests. Finally, I describe a study where we attempted to investigate specific aspects of conceptual processing that may be contributing to the implicit memory bias in depression (Watkins, Grimm, May, Krueger, & Whitney, 2000a). Although our findings were not as we predicted and were somewhat equivocal, implicit memory bias was shown in one of the two conceptually driven tests. Throughout this discussion I will review findings from other laboratories that speak to the issue of implicit memory bias in depression. The focus of my review will be on processes that appear to be involved both at study and test in the demonstration of implicit memory bias in depression. I will attempt to show that conceptual processing is necessary both at study and at test for implicit memory bias to be shown.

However, I will also present data supporting the proposition that conceptual processing is not sufficient for producing implicit memory bias in depression.

IMPLICIT MEMORY BIAS IN WORD STEM COMPLETION

The first question we attempted to answer in my laboratory was: Is there an implicit memory bias in depression? It will become clear that this question was simplistic, but my colleagues and I first attempted to investigate implicit memory bias in depression by using a word stem completion task (Watkins et al., 1992). As I described earlier, in word stem completion the participant is asked to produce the first word that comes to mind beginning with three or four letters. In this study our participants studied positive, depressive relevant (e.g., hopeless, guilty, foolish, inferior, etc.), neutral, and physical threat (e.g., suffocate, coronary, stab) words in an imaginal self-referent task. In this encoding task participants were provided with a study word and were asked to imagine themselves in a scene involving a referent of the word. After study, participants completed both an implicit and an explicit memory test, counterbalanced for order. Both tests used letter stems for retrieval cues and only differed in the instructions. In the implicit test the participants were told to produce the first word that comes to mind beginning with the letter stems and in the explicit test participants were instructed to attempt to produce words from the study list that began with the letters provided. In explicit memory, we found the expected MCM effect. However, we found that the explicit memory bias did not extend to all negative words, only the depression-relevant words. Physically threatening words did not show any differences between groups. Contrasting with the explicit memory findings, no implicit memory bias was found. In addition, no priming deficit was evident in depressed participants.

Denny and Hunt (1992) conducted a very similar study to ours but used free recall as their explicit test and word fragment completion as their implicit test. In word fragment completion the participant is provided with several letters of the word and blanks for the missing letters (e.g., p__c_f_l, for *peaceful*) and they are asked to produce the first word that comes to mind. Like our study, Denny and Hunt found the expected MCM bias in explicit memory, but no implicit memory bias. Although the theories of Beck (e.g., Beck, Rush, Shaw & Emery, 1979) and Bower (e.g., 1981) are silent with regard to predictions about implicit memory, both theories seem to imply that with depression or sadness, negative or mood-congruent information should be more activated and thus more accessible regardless of the retrieval task used (cf. Bower & Forgas, 2000). The findings of Denny and Hunt (1992) and Watkins et al. (1992) do not support this assumption, however. The contrasting results of implicit and explicit memory in these studies suggests that it is not simply that negative information is more activated in depressed mood, but that how this information is accessed also matters.

These studies appeared to show that MCM depended at least in part on the type of retrieval task used. Although the theories of Bower or Beck did not predict these results, they fit nicely with the predictions offered by the original theory of Williams, Watts, MacLeod, and Mathews (1988). Following Graf and Mandler (1984), Williams et al. posited two distinct cognitive processes that may be differentially biased by different emotional states and disorders. An initial integration or priming stage is automatic and occurs because components of a stimulus are mutually activated. Because of mutual activation of the stimulus components, the stimulus becomes more integrated. The more integrated a stimulus is, the more likely the entire stimulus will be accessed if some of its components are activated. However, in Graf and Mandler's words, although an item may be more accessible because it is more integrated, it will not necessarily be more retrievable. According to Graf and Mandler, a word will only be more retrievable in explicit memory if it is more elaborated. Elaboration refers to the "activation of a representation in relation to other associated representations to form new relationships between them and to activate old relationships" (Williams et al., 1988, p. 170). Elaboration makes a word more retrievable because it provides more complete routes of access to the representation. Williams et al. proposed that mood-congruent processes in depression took place more at the elaboration stage than the more automatic integration stage (which they referred to as the priming stage). Results from explicit tests are said to be more reflective of elaborative processes, while implicit memory tests result from integration. Thus, the finding of MCM on an explicit memory test, but not on an implicit test, provides support for this approach.

However, there are alternative approaches to the implicit/explicit memory distinction offered by Graf and Mandler (1984). Roediger and McDermott (1992) provided an interesting commentary on the results of Denny and Hunt (1992) and Watkins et al. (1992). They observed that a transfer appropriate processing approach (TAP; Morris, Bransford & Franks, 1977, see also Blaxton, 1989, 1995; Roediger, 1990) would also predict this pattern of data. In brief, TAP theory states that if the cognitive processes activated at study are recapitulated at test, then a studied item will be more likely to be retrieved. Thus, when similar cognitive processes at study and test are activated, the transfer is "appropriate" and memory benefits. Although study and test tasks likely involve many component cognitive processes, TAP theory advocates have tended to emphasise the distinction between perceptual and conceptual processes. Thus, perceptually driven tasks are those in which perceptual processes are most important. For example, in the word stem completion test participants are responding to the perceptual features of the stems (e.g., fai___) rather than to their meaning. On the other hand, conceptually driven tasks are those that require participants to attend to the meaning of the cues presented, not their perceptual features. A free recall test is conceptually driven because the participant must meaningfully relate the test instructions to the study task. Thus, the

TAP approach argues that if conceptual processes are activated at study, then studied items will be more likely to be retrieved if the test also activates conceptual processes. However, if conceptual processes are activated at study but perceptual processes are required by the test, retrieval of study items will not be likely. In Denny and Hunt, and in Watkins et al. (1992), conceptual processing was activated at study but perceptual processing was emphasised at test.

Blaxton, Roediger, and colleagues have pointed out that virtually all explicit tests are conceptually driven, while most implicit tests used before 1990 were perceptually driven. Most implicit tests use degraded perceptual stimuli and the participant is asked to complete the cue without any reference to the study material. Thus, many implicit memory studies confound implicit and explicit memory with perceptual and conceptual processes. This confound was also evident in Denny and Hunt (1992) and Watkins et al. (1992). Roediger and McDermott (1992) stated that the results of these two studies were not surprising because MCM requires participants to retrieve different types of words based on their meaning. Because word stem completion is a perceptually driven test, MCM would not be expected because conceptual processes were not required. The critical insight here appears to be that MCM will only be found if conceptual elaboration takes place at study, and at test, and this is the hypothesis that the following studies tested. Note that one need only argue that the meaning of the stimulus must be accessed at both study and test, not necessarily that conceptual elaboration must be transfer appropriate.

Following Roediger and McDermott's approach, one would not expect an implicit MCM bias when perceptually driven tests are used. However, Roediger has pointed out that implicit tests need not be perceptually driven. One can create tests that are unintentional, but require the participant to activate conceptual processes (e.g., Blaxton, 1989). Roediger and McDermott (1992) predicted that if a conceptually driven implicit memory test is used, then MCM would be found. This is what we set out to investigate in our next project.

CONCEPTUALLY DRIVEN IMPLICIT MEMORY BIAS

In our next study (Watkins et al., 1996) we set out to answer the question: Is there a conceptual implicit memory bias in depression? The conceptual test we chose to use was free association. Through pilot work we chose a number of association cues that were moderately related to our targets. In the actual study participants were first randomly assigned to study one of two sets of target words we had created. Each set contained positive, negative, and neutral words. Participants studied the words using the imaginal self-referent task we used in the first study. After imagining each scene, participants were asked several questions about the scene. They were asked: (1) whether the scene was an actual scene from their past or an imagined scene, (2) whether they were the principal character of the scene, (3) to rate the vividness of the scene, and (4) to rate the pleasantness-unpleasantness of the scene. Clearly, this encoding task required considerable conceptual elaboration. Following a filler task, participants were then administered the free association task which contained association cues that were related to target words from both studied and unstudied word sets. Priming was revealed by subtracting the number of unstudied targets from the number of studied targets produced. Priming was shown to be robust, and we found a significant interaction between group, priming, and valence, indicating an implicit MCM bias as predicted by Roediger and McDermott (1992). As can be seen in Figure 1, controls performance for positive words showed more than twice the priming results of depressed participants, and conversely the priming performance by depressed individuals was over twice that of controls for negative words. Thus, it appears that an implicit memory bias may exist in depression if conceptual processes are activated.

The work of Bradley and Mogg also lends support to the contention that conceptual processes are important to an implicit memory bias in depression. In two studies (Bradley, Mogg, & Millar, 1996; Bradley, Mogg, & Williams,

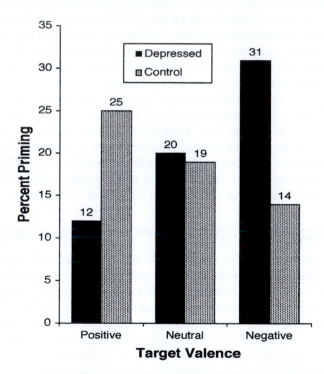

Figure 1.   Per cent priming by group and valence in free association implicit test. (Adapted from "Unconscious mood-congruent memory bias in depression" by Watkins, Vache, Verney, Muller, and Mathews, 1996, *Journal of Abnormal Psychology*, *105*, p. 39. Copyright © 1996 by the American Psychological Association and adapted with permission from the authors.)

1995), they have demonstrated an implicit MCM bias in depression with a lexical decision task (see also Bradley, Mogg, & Williams, 1994 and Scott, Mogg, & Bradley, 2001, for similar results with nonclinical populations). In lexical decision, participants responding faster in identifying a stimulus as a word (versus a nonword) to studied than to unstudied words demonstrates implicit memory. These studies were intriguing because they demonstrated an implicit memory bias with both suprathreshold and subthreshold priming. In other words, some words were studied consciously, and others were presented too briefly for conscious identification (14 ms). Although one might question whether lexical decision should be viewed as a conceptually driven test (cf. Roediger & McDermott, 1993), it seems that in this task participants had to pay attention to the meaning of the word at some level in order to identify it as a word. This is because the nonwords that were used in their lexical decision task were pronounceable, and so the participant could not rely on perceptual features to make their decisions. Second, semantic variables are known to affect lexical decision (e.g., Neely, 1977). Third, in these studies Bradley and colleagues presented the primes in uppercase letters and the targets in the lexical decision task in lower case letters. The words from study to test were perceptually mismatched and thus it was unlikely that the priming was due to perceptual transfer. These studies lend more credence to the conclusion that conceptual processes are important to implicit memory bias in depression.

COMPARING PERCEPTUAL AND CONCEPTUAL PROCESSES IN IMPLICIT MEMORY BIAS

We were tempted to interpret these data as clear evidence that implicit MCM bias would be found if conceptual processes were activated but not with perceptual processes. However, there were several issues preventing us from making this strong conclusion. Although by now several studies had failed to find an implicit memory bias in depression using perceptually driven tests (Bazin, Perruchet, De Bonis, & Feline, 1994; Danion, Kauffmann-Muller, Grange, Zimmermann, & Greth. 1995; Ilsley, Moffoot, & O'Carroll, 1995), and our finding of a conceptually driven implicit bias was compelling, there are several problems with comparing results from different studies. It could be that different results were found because of different subject populations, or different experimental word stimuli used, or a host of other inter-study differences. Thus, we decided to directly compare perceptually driven and conceptually driven tests in the same study.

In our next project (Watkins et al., 2000b), we sought to investigate the boundary conditions of implicit MCM. By directly comparing the contribution of perceptual and conceptual processes, we hoped to show that conceptual processes were required to show an implicit MCM bias. In previous studies we had not manipulated processing at encoding, all participants encoded the words through conceptual elaboration. In the present study we further tested assumptions of TAP by manipulating encoding within subjects. Participants studied positive and negative words either by counting the number of ascending and descending letters in a word (a structural or perceptually driven task), or by rating the recency of their experience with the word on a Likert type scale (a task requiring conceptual processing of the study word). Following two filler tasks, participants completed one of four different implicit memory tests. Each test contained cues for targets that had been studied and also for nonstudied targets. Two of the tests were chosen because of their perceptually driven nature, and two because they appeared to meet the criteria for conceptually driven tests. The two perceptually driven tests were word stem completion and word identification (sometimes known as perceptual identification). In word identification participants were exposed to each word for a very short duration (33 ms), followed by a mask, and then the participant was asked to read the word. In this task, participants often complained that they did not see the word, but still were able to read more studied than nonstudied words showing the effect of implicit memory (Feustal, Shiffrin, & Salasoo, 1983; Jacoby & Dallas, 1981). The two conceptually driven implicit tests we used were free association and semantic definition. The free association task was identical to the one described previously, except that we limited the number of associations participants produced to each cue to three, rather than giving them a time limit for each cue as before. Semantic definition was a somewhat novel task that we adopted from the semantic priming literature (e.g., Bowles & Poon, 1985; Brown, 1979, 1981). In this task we provided participants with a definition and the first letter of a word, and asked them to produce a word that began with the letter provided and that fit the definition. Although this task contains a perceptual component (first letter of the target word), priming with perceptually encoded words was not reliable in this task, and so transfer was primarily determined by conceptual processes. Definitions of both studied and nonstudied words were administered to our participants. We found that this measure produced good priming for conceptually studied words. Both free association and semantic definition are conceptual because the participant must attend to the meaning, not merely the perceptual features, of the cues. Table 1 shows examples of cues for the four different implicit tests for the target "confident".

Following Roediger and McDermott (1992), we predicted that there would be no evidence of MCM in the perceptually driven tests. Conversely we predicted that an implicit MCM bias would be demonstrated in both conceptually driven tests, but only with words that were conceptually encoded. Our data analytic approach was to analyse perceptually encoded and conceptually encoded words separately, which allowed us to compare new items to each type of previously processed item (i.e., the priming effect for perceptually processed words in one analysis, and the priming effect for conceptually processed words in another

TABLE 1
Examples of implicit test cues for the target "Confident"

Perceptually driven		Conceptually driven	
Word stem completion	Perceptual identification	Free association	Semantic definition
Complete this stem with the first word that comes to mind: con_____.	Subjects see a word flashed very quickly on the computer screen (33 ms), and are asked to identify the word.	Produce three one-word associations to this cue: Assured	What word fits the following definition? A belief in oneself, one's abilities, and the likelihood of success. c_____.

Source: Watkins et al. (2000b).

analysis). As we predicted, the interaction between priming, group, word valence, and test was not statistically reliable for perceptually encoded words ($F < 1.0$). Regardless of the implicit test used, we found no evidence for a reliable implicit MCM bias when words were studied with respect to their perceptual features. However, when participants were forced to attend to the meaning of the word during study, a different pattern emerged. The priming × group × word valence × test interaction for conceptually studied words was shown to be statistically reliable. To interpret this interaction, we then conducted priming × group × word valence analyses for each implicit memory test. Our predictions were supported for the perceptually driven tests. No reliable implicit MCM bias was found in word stem completion or in the word identification test ($Fs < 1.0$). In fact, the pattern of priming means for conceptually encoded words in the word identification test was mood-incongruent. In a similar study using word identification following either perceptual or conceptual processing tasks, Hertel (1994) also failed to find any evidence of implicit MCM with clinically depressed individuals.

Our findings with regard to the conceptually driven tests were mixed. In the semantic definition test, the group × priming × word valence interaction was statistically reliable, indicating an implicit MCM bias with conceptually enco-ded words as we had predicted. Figure 2 shows this finding and reveals a rather robust mood-congruent effect with conceptually encoded words. In this figure, the priming results for perceptually encoded words are shown on the left side of the graph, and those for conceptually studied words are shown on the right. However, contrary to predictions—and in direct contrast to Watkins et al. (1996)—no MCM bias was found in the free association test (group × priming × word valence: $F < 1.0$). In fact, the priming means did not show the slightest conformity to a mood-congruent pattern. This result presented a significant

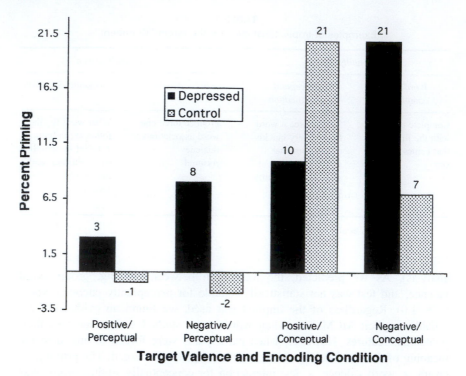

Figure 2. Per cent priming by group, valence, and encoding condition in semantic definition implicit test. (Adapted from ''Unconscious memory bias in depression: Perceptual and conceptual processes'' by Watkins, Martin, and Stern, 2000, *Journal of Abnormal Psychology*, *109*, p. 286. Copyright © 2000 by the American Psychological Association and adapted with permission from the authors.)

interpretation challenge—as our earlier finding with almost an identical implicit measure seemed so strong.

There are several procedural differences between the method used by Watkins et al. (1996) and the method in our more recent study (Watkins et al., 2000b). First, in Watkins et al. (1996) we used an encoding task which involved much more conceptual elaboration than the recency rating task used by Watkins et al. (2000b). Second, in the free association task, Watkins et al. (1996) required the participants to produce as many associations related to the cue as possible in 30 s, but in Watkins et al. (2000b) participants were limited to three associations per cue. It is possible that in our more recent study participants were more concerned with quickly producing three associations to proceed to the next trial and thus finish the study more quickly. This may have resulted in less conceptual elaboration of the association cue than was the case in Watkins et al. (1996). If this is true, it is possible that words produced in the former study were more meaningfully related to the association cues than in Watkins et al. (2000b). Although the free association task clearly falls into the conceptually driven category, it could be argued that the free association task used in this study required less conceptual processing than that used in Watkins et al. (1996). General priming data appeared to support this suggestion. Overall priming levels for free association in the Watkins et al. (1996) study were 19.17%, but dropped to 7.82% for conceptually encoded words in the more recent study (Watkins et al. (2000b). Others have questioned the conceptually driven nature of free association. For example, after experiencing similar difficulties with their free association test, Weldon and Coyote (1996) suggested that free association might actually tap lexical access more than conceptual processing. Thus, it is possible that although conceptual processes affected our free association test, it required less conceptual processing than the semantic definition test.

The dissociation between our conceptual tests highlights the fact that it is unlikely that all conceptually driven tests "are created equal". The TAP approach as derived by Roediger (e.g., Roediger & McDermott, 1993), tends to emphasise the form of the initial processing of the test cues. In this regard both free association and semantic definition are clearly conceptually driven because participants must attend to the meaning of the cues. However, in each memory task there are several cognitive operations, each of which may or may not require conceptual processing. In both free association and semantic definition tests the participant is required to attend to the meaning of the retrieval cues. However, in the free association test the participant is not required to attend to the meaning of the word produced whereas in the semantic definition test they are. For example, in the free association test when a participant produces associations to the cue "Assured", they need not be overly concerned with the meaning of the words they produce. However, for semantic definition, the participant is administered a definition and the word they produce must be appropriate for the definition. For example, when participants see the definition "A belief in oneself, one's abilities, and the likelihood of success", the meaning of the word they produce must be attended to. In this regard TAP theory would appear to benefit from some fine-tuning of the component processes that different implicit tests may require. A starting point would be to define component processes involved in the initial attention to the retrieval cue, and processes involved with target production.

To reiterate the findings of Watkins et al. (2000b), we found no evidence for implicit memory bias in the perceptually driven tests, and an implicit MCM bias in one of the two conceptually driven tests, but only with conceptually encoded words. Although an argument could be made about the conceptually driven nature of the free association test, it clearly meets the specifications as defined by Roediger (Roediger & McDermott, 1993). Further, a levels-of-processing effect was demonstrated on this measure, which is one of the defining characteristics of conceptually driven tests. My conjectures above regarding the conceptually driven nature of free association are *post-hoc*, and many other interpretations are possible. Not only did this study show a dissociation between perceptually driven and conceptually driven tests, there was also a dissociation between the two conceptually driven implicit tests. Thus, conceptually driven processing does not ensure MCM bias. As Colin MacLeod observed (personal communication, May 1999), conceptual processing appears to be necessary, but not sufficient for producing implicit memory bias in depression. Questions remained as to what specific conceptual processes were required to produce implicit MCM bias.

SELF-REFERENCE AND IMPLICIT MEMORY BIAS

In re-evaluating the findings from Watkins et al., (2000b), we discovered that we had inadvertently used personal pronouns in 42% of the definitions in the semantic definition test. It is possible that our semantic definition test actually activated self-referent processing. Was self-referent processing the specific conceptual process supporting implicit memory bias in depression? In Watkins et al. (2000b), our encoding task was not only conceptual, but self-referential as well. Furthermore, if one implicit test was more self-referential than the other, the TAP approach would predict more transfer of learning to that test. Could it be that we inadvertently manipulated self-referent processing in our two conceptual tests? This is the idea we sought to test in our most recent study (Watkins, et al., 2000a). Several studies have suggested that in explicit memory, self-referent processing is more likely to produce MCM (e.g., Mathews & Bradley, 1983). Could this be the case with implicit memory as well? In our most recent study we attempted to investigate the question, Are self-referent processes required to demonstrate implicit MCM bias in depression?

In this study we attempted to manipulate self-reference at both study and test. Participants encoded positive and negative words by imagining themselves involved in a situation with the referent of the word (self-reference), or rating which of six cartoon drawings of somewhat ambiguous situations best fit the word. After completing two filler tasks, participants were assigned to one of two implicit tests. The tests were very similar to the semantic definition task used in Watkins et al. (2000b) in that we provided participants with definitions and the first letter of the target appropriate to the definition. However, the definitions were provided in more of a sentence completion format and we attempted to manipulate self-reference between the two implicit tests. In the self-referent test every definition included a personal pronoun, for example, "When others are thankful for my contribution I may feel a_____ by them" (*appreciated*). In the other-referent condition all of the sentences made reference to an ambiguous character named Peter, for example, "When Peter receives thanks for his contribution he may feel a_____". We elected to make this a between-subjects variable because we felt that exposing both types of cues to the same subject might cause some leaking of self- and other-referent processes across trials. Following TAP theory, we predicted that implicit MCM would be found only in the self-referent test, and only with words encoded with reference to the self.

Our results were not as predicted, and were somewhat equivocal. We followed the data analytic approach of Watkins et al. (2000b) in analysing results for the two levels of encoding separately. For words encoded in the other-referent condition, an implicit MCM bias was found regardless of the type of test used, Group × Valence × Priming: $F(1, 98) = 3.95$, $p < .05$. In other words, an implicit MCM pattern was found in both of the implicit tests (self-referent and other-referent), for words that were studied with respect to the ambiguous cartoon characters. Figure 3 shows this finding by collapsing the results from the two implicit memory tests. We did not predict these results because we felt that other-referent encoding would not support an implicit memory bias. However, this result is consistent with the theory that conceptual processing is required to demonstrate implicit MCM. Results from the self-referent encoded words were equivocal. The group × valence × priming × test interaction failed to reach significance, $F(1, 98) = 2.21$, $p = .14$. Here the trend of the result was a mood-incongruent pattern in the other-referent test and a mood-congruent trend in the

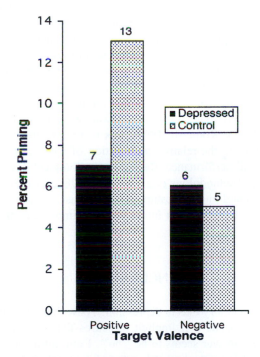

Figure 3. Per cent priming by group and valence for other-referent encoded words in sentence completion implicit test.

self-referent test. Although this pattern conforms to TAP predictions, clearly the most interpretable result comes from the other-referent encoded words, a finding we did not predict.

One potential problem with this study might have been that our self-reference manipulation was not strong enough. It is unclear exactly how participants made their judgements in the other-referent encoding task. Because they were relating words to an ambiguous cartoon character, it could be argued that the way they made this decision was by applying the character to themselves. However, if this were the case, both encoding conditions should have revealed the same result, which was not the case. Future researchers might want to make a clearer self and other reference manipulation, both at study and at test. It is also possible that the other-referent encoding condition was less constrained and so allowed for more mood-congruent elaboration.

It is now known that explicit processes can be involved with implicit tests (Jacoby, 1991; Jacoby, Lindsay, & Toth, 1992; Jacoby, Toth, & Yonelinas, 1993), and it is possible that participants were explicitly recollecting study materials during the implicit test. For example, it is possible that on items where a word did not immediately come to mind fitting the sentence, participants developed a strategy to consciously search words that they had learned from the study task. This could also be a problem with the two other studies that demonstrated implicit MCM. However, memory awareness interview data in all of these studies does not support this interpretation. They showed that participants rarely reported using conscious recollection (usually under 5%), and about half of the participants did not realise that they had even produced words from the study task. Although the *process dissociation* approach developed by L. L. Jacoby (e.g., 1991) may make estimates that are too conservative regarding the contribution of unconscious processes (Cowan & Stadler, 1996; Dodson & Johnson, 1996; Graf & Komatsu, 1994), this technique appears to be the best available for evaluating the relative contribution of conscious and unconscious processes to retrieval performance. Recent methodological developments in the process dissociation methodology (e.g., Jacoby, 1998; Stern, Sagerser, Becic, & McBride, 2001), should improve estimates of unconscious processes. Use of the process dissociation framework in future work on implicit memory bias should be informative.

CONCLUSIONS

Is there an implicit memory bias in depression? As with many things, the answer appears to be "it depends". If implicit measures that rely on perceptual processes are used, the answer seems to be "no". I am not aware of any study of clinically depressed individuals that has found an implicit memory bias when perceptually driven tests are used. I should state, however, that priming means in both of our studies using word stem completion were in the mood-congruent direction (Watkins et al., 1992; Watkins et al., 2000b). This also seems to be the case in other studies that have investigated implicit memory bias in depression with this test (Bazin et al., 1994; Danion et al., 1995; Ilsley et al., 1995; see also Denny & Hunt, 1992, with word fragment completion). However, none of these studies found anything close to a statistically reliable implicit memory bias, so the conclusion that there is no implicit memory bias in depression when perceptually driven tests are used, seems to be fairly safe. On the other hand, our research has shown that implicit MCM can be demonstrated if conceptually driven tests are used. In three studies we have demonstrated a conceptually driven implicit memory bias (Watkins et al., 1996, Watkins et al., 2000b). It should be noted that in Watkins, Martin, and Stern, implicit memory bias was found only in the semantic definition test, and only when words were studied conceptually. Thus, it appears that conceptual processing is necessary at study and at test for implicit MCM to occur. However, twice we have used conceptually driven tests and have failed to show a statistically reliable memory bias. In fact, the free association test used by Watkins et al. (2000b) showed no evidence of mood-congruence. Although I have attempted to offer some explanations as to why we failed to find MCM on these occasions, these explanations are *post-hoc* and currently have no direct empirical support. One account of these varying results is simply that the implicit memory bias in conceptually driven tests is inconsistent. The priming methodology is fraught with many pitfalls, and it appears that other laboratories have found this effect to be somewhat fickle as well (cf. Scott et al., 2001). When one is dealing with priming effects between 10% and 20%, it seems that sources of error variance could easily affect the outcome on these measures. In this regard, I believe the field would benefit from the development of more sensitive priming measures, and more standardised valenced word sets. Concerning the latter issue, we have found across studies several positive words that were more easily primed for depressives than controls (e.g., cherished, fulfilled, needed, and relieved; Whitney, Watkins, & May, 2000). Although it might lower the generalisability of the MCM effect, using standard word sets that produce reliable memory biases should assist researchers investigating specific processes involved with MCM. Despite the inconsistency of findings, this should not detract from the conclusion that conceptual processes seem to be required for implicit MCM bias to be demonstrated in depression. Thus, it appears that conceptual processing is necessary, but is not sufficient for implicit memory bias in depression to occur.

Although TAP theory has been a helpful framework for explaining mood-congruent patterns in depression, several of our findings were not predicted by the TAP approach. TAP theory would likely benefit from further distinctions within the conceptual processing domain. As Roediger and McDermott (1993) point out, the distinction between perceptual and conceptual processes "is likely too rough" (p. 118), and further refinement of the theory and of component processes of study and test tasks would appear to improve the predictive power of TAP.

An overview of the data from my laboratory supports the idea that as conceptual elaboration increases at study and test, implicit MCM bias in depression is more likely to be observed. The practical relevance of these findings is highlighted by the work of Nolen-Hoeksema, who has demonstrated that rumination is an important cognitive component of depression (e.g., Nolen-Hoeksema, 1991, 2000; Nolen-Hoeksema, Morrow, & Fredrickson, 1993; for a review see Nolen-Hoeksema, 1987). It seems appropriate to conclude that by definition, rumination involves the conceptual elaboration of unpleasant thoughts and memories. As a depressed person ruminates on unpleasant information, they are engaging in mood-congruent conceptual elaboration. Not only does this make the information more available to both explicit and implicit retrieval, elaborating this information in a mood-congruent fashion should also serve to enhance explicit and implicit retrieval of information related to this material. Retrieval of additional unpleasant information might only provide the subject material for more rumination. Recent evidence has suggested that mood may not affect memory in the direct way suggested by seminal cognition and emotion theories (e.g., Bower, 1981). For example, McFarland and Buehler (1998) found that when participants attended to their induced mood in a reflective manner, a mood-incongruent recall pattern resulted. However, when attention to mood was in a ruminative fashion, the expected mood-congruent result was found. This result implies that individual differences and aspects of the depressed state that promote conceptual elaborative processing will also promote implicit and explicit MCM. The identification of these factors by future research would appear to be important to issues of prevention and intervention for depression.

Further, the approach of Fox, Russo, and Dutton (this issue) may be helpful in interpreting the data from my laboratory. The failure to disengage attention from negative concepts may be a useful explanation for the tendency of depressives to elaborate on mood-congruent information. Whatever the case, it appears fairly clear that the processing of meaningful aspects of stimuli at both study and test is necessary for implicit memory bias to be observed. This pattern of conceptual elaboration may not be the case with other emotional disorders however. A number of studies have demonstrated an implicit MCM bias with anxiety disorders using word stem completion, a perceptually driven implicit memory test (e.g., MacLeod, & McLaughlin 1995; Mathews, Mogg May, & Eysenck, 1989). One interpretation of the implicit memory results in anxiety is that mood-congruence is limited to perceptual processing, or at least to pre-attentive conceptual processing. It appears that mood-congruent biases do not occur at all levels of cognitive processing in depression, and different emotional states show mood-congruence at different levels of cognitive processing. Successful cognitive theories of the emotional disorders will have to take this pattern of results into account.

I began this review by suggesting that an implicit memory bias might be a more important maintenance mechanism of depression than an explicit memory bias. It appears, however, that explicit memory biases are more consistently demonstrated in the literature (Blaney, 1986). It could be that the apparent implicit/explicit memory bias differences in consistency are due to methodological differences, rather than to differences between implicit and explicit memory *per se*. This is an issue that must be left to future research. But as the results stand to date, the more consistent bias appears to be in explicit conscious recollection, rather than in implicit unintentional retrieval. If MCM bias is an important maintenance mechanism in depression, the greater consistency of explicit memory bias findings leads to the suggestion that an explicit memory bias may be more important to the maintenance of depression than an implicit bias. This proposal is consistent with the approach of Williams et al. (1988, Williams, Watts, MacLeod, & Mathews, 1997), in that conscious, strategic mood-congruent elaboration is the more likely culprit underlying negative thinking biases in depression. I would submit that the studies reviewed here show that mood-congruence in depression is not limited to conscious elaboration, but clearly, conceptual elaboration is necessary for either explicit or implicit MCM bias to occur. The interpretation that conscious mood-congruent elaboration is the more important maintenance mechanism in depression may be good news for depression practitioners. Because psychological treatments largely use conscious intervention techniques, it would appear that an explicit MCM bias would be more amenable to treatment than an implicit memory bias. Whatever the case, research has yet to determine if memory biases directly contribute to the maintenance of depression, and if so, whether direct intervention with memory bias alleviates depression.

Manuscript received 15 October 2000
Revised manuscript received 23 May 2001

REFERENCES

Bazin, N., Perruchet, P., De Bonis, M., & Feline, A. (1994). The dissociation of explicit and implicit memory in depressed patients. *Psychological Medicine, 24*, 238–245.

Beck, A.T., Rush, A.J., Shaw, B.F., & Emery, G. (1979). *Cognitive therapy of depression*. New York: Guilford Press.

Blaney, P.H. (1986). Affect and memory: A review. *Psychological Bulletin, 99*, 229–246.

Blaxton, T.A. (1989). Investigating dissociations among memory measures: Support for a transfer-appropriate processing framework. *Journal of Experimental Psychology, Learning, Memory, and Cognition, 15*, 657–668.

Blaxton, T.A. (1995). A process-based view of memory. *Journal of International Neuropsychological Society, 1*, 112–114.

Bower, G.H. (1981). Mood and memory. *American Psychologist, 36*, 129–148.

Bower, G.H., & Forgas, J.P. (2000). Affect, memory, and social cognition. In E. Eich, J.F. Kihlstrom, G.H. Bower, J.P. Forgas, & P.M. Niedenthal (Eds.), *Cognition and emotion* (p. 87–168). Oxford, UK: Oxford University Press.

Bowles, N.L., & Poon, L.W. (1985). Effects of priming in word retrieval. *Journal of Experimental Psychology: Learning, Memory, and Cognition, 11*, 272–283.

Bradley, B.P., Mogg, K., & Millar (1996). Implicit memory bias in clinical and non-clinical depression. *Behaviour Research and Therapy, 34*, 865–879.

Bradley, B.P., Mogg, K., & Williams, R. (1994). Implicit and explicit memory for emotional information in non-clinical subjects. *Behaviour Research and Therapy, 32*, 65–78.

Bradley, B.P., Mogg, K., & Williams, R. (1995). Implicit and explicit memory for emotion-congruent information in clinical depression and anxiety. *Behaviour Research and Therapy, 33*, 755–770.

Brown, A.S. (1979). Priming effects in semantic memory retrieval processes. *Journal of Experimental Psychology: Human Learning and Memory, 5*, 65–77.

Brown, A.S. (1981). Inhibition in cued retrieval. *Journal of Experimental Psychology: Human Learning and Memory, 7*, 204–215.

Cowan, N., & Stadler, M.A. (1996). Estimating unconscious processes: Implications of a general class of models. *Journal of Experimental Psychology: General, 125*, 195–200.

Danion, J., Kauffmann-Muller, F., Grange, D., Zimmermann, M., & Greth, G. (1995). Affective valence of words, explicit and implicit memory in clinical depression. *Journal of Affective Disorders, 34*, 227–234.

Denny, E.R., & Hunt, R.R. (1992). Affective valence and memory in depression: Dissociation of recall and fragment completion. *Journal of Abnormal Psychology, 101*, 575–580.

Dodson, C.S., & Johnson, M.K. (1996). Some problems with the process dissociation approach to memory. *Journal of Experimental Psychology: General, 125*, 181–194.

Feustal, T.C., Shiffrin, R.M., & Salasoo, A. (1983). Episodic and lexical contributions to the repetition effect in word recognition. *Journal of Experimental Psychology: General, 112*, 309–346.

Graf, P., & Komatsu, S. (1994). Process dissociation procedure: Handle with caution! *European Journal of Cognitive Psychology, 6*, 113–129.

Graf, P., & Mandler, G. (1984). Activation makes words more accessible, but not necessarily more retrievable. *Journal of Verbal Learning and Behavior, 23*, 553–568.

Hertel, P.T. (1994). Depressive deficits in word identification and recall. *Cognition and Emotion, 8*, 313–327.

Ilsley, J.E., Moffoot, A.P.R., & O'Carroll, R.E. (1995). An analysis of memory dysfunction in major depression. *Journal of Affective Disorders, 35*, 1–9.

Jacoby, L.L. (1991). A process dissociation framework: Separating automatic and intentional uses of memory. *Journal of Memory and Language, 30*, 513–541.

Jacoby, L.L. (1998). Invariance of automatic influences in memory: Toward a user's guide for the process dissociation procedure. *Journal of Experimental Psychology: Learning, Memory, and Cognition, 24*, 3–26.

Jacoby, L.L., & Dallas, M. (1981). On the relationship between autobiographical memory and perceptual learning. *Journal of Experimental Psychology: General, 110*, 306–340.

Jacoby, L.L., Lindsay, D.S., & Toth, J.P. (1992). Unconscious influences revealed: Attention, awareness, and control. *American Psychologist, 47*, 802–809.

Jacoby, L.L., Toth, J.P., & Yonelinas, A.P. (1993). Unconscious influences of memory: Dissociations and automaticity. *Journal of Experimental Psychology: General, 122*, 139–154.

MacLeod, C., & McLaughlin, K. (1995). Implicit and explicit memory bias in anxiety: A conceptual replication. *Behaviour Research and Therapy, 33*, 1–14.

Mason, M.E., & Graf, P. (1993). Introduction: Looking back and into the future. In P. Graf & E.J. Masson (Eds.), *Implicit memory: New directions in cognition, development, and neuropsychology* (pp. 1–11). Hillsdale, NJ: Erlbaum.

Mathews, A., & Bradley, B. (1983). Mood and the self-reference bias in recall. *Behaviour Research and Therapy, 21*, 233–239.

Mathews, A., Mogg, K., May, J., & Eysenck, M. (1989). Implicit and explicit memory bias in anxiety. *Journal of Abnormal Psychology, 98*, 236–240.

McFarland, C., & Buehler, R. (1998). The impact of negative affect on autobiographical memory: The role of self-focused attention to moods. *Journal of Personality and Social Psychology, 75*, 1424–1440.

Morris, C.D., Bransford, J.D., & Franks, J.J. (1977). Levels of processing versus transfer-appropriate processing. *Journal of Verbal Learning and Verbal Behavior, 16*, 519–533.

Neely, J.H. (1977). Semantic priming and retrieval from lexical memory: Roles of inhibitionless spreading activation and limited-capacity attention. *Journal of Experimental Psychology: General, 106*, 226–254.

Nelson, D.L. (1979). Remembering picture and words: Appearance, significance, and name. In L.S. Cermack & F.I.M. Craik (Eds.), *Levels of processing in human memory* (pp. 45–76). Hillsdale, NJ: Erlbaum.

Nolen-Hoeksema, S. (1987). Sex differences in depression: Evidence and theory. *Psychological Bulletin, 101*, 259–282.

Nolen-Hoeksema, S. (1991). Responses to depression and their effects on the duration of depressive episodes. *Journal of Abnormal Psychology, 100*, 569–582.

Nolen-Hoeksema, S. (2000). The role of rumination in depressive disorders and mixed anxiety/depressive symptoms. *Journal of Abnormal Psychology, 109*, 504–511.

Nolen-Hoeksema, S., Morrow, J., & Fredrickson, B. (1993). Response styles and the duration of episodes of depressed mood. *Journal of Abnormal Psychology, 102*, 20–28.

Novo, M.J. , & Watkins, P.C. (2000, June). *Cognitive symptoms of depression as predictors of unconscious mood-congruent memory bias.* Presentation at the 12th Annual Convention of the American Psychological Society, Miami Beach, FL.

Richardson-Klavehn, A., Lee, M.G., Joubran, R., & Bjork, R.A. (1994). Intention and awareness in perceptual identification priming. *Memory and Cognition, 22*, 293–312.

Roediger, H.L. (1990). Implicit memory: Retention without remembering. *American Psychologist, 45*, 1043–1056.

Roediger, H.L. & McDermott, K.B. (1992). Depression and implicit memory: A commentary. *Journal of Abnormal Psychology, 101*, 587–591.

Roediger, H.L., & McDermott, K.B. (1993). Implicit memory in normal human subjects. In F. Boller & J. Grafman (Eds.), *Handbook of neuropsychology* (pp. 63–131). Amsterdam: Elsevier.

Schacter, D.L. (1987). Implicit memory: History and current status. *Journal of Experimental Psychology: Learning, Memory, and Cognition, 13*, 501–518.

Schacter, D.L. (1990). Introduction to "Implicit memory: Multiple perspectives". *Bulletin of the Psychonomic Society, 28*, 338–340.

Scott, K.M., Mogg, K., & Bradley, B. (2001). Masked semantic priming of emotional information in subclinical depression. *Cognitive Therapy and Research, 25*, 505–524.

Smith, E.R., & Branscombe, N.R. (1988). Category accessibility as implicit memory. *Journal of Experimental Social Psychology, 24*, 490–504.

Smith, M.C., & Magee, L.E. (1980). Tracing the time course of picture-word processing. *Journal of Experimental Psychology: General, 109*, 373–392.

Srull, T.K., & Wyer, R.S. (1979). The role of category accessibility in the interpretation of information about persons: Some determinants and implications. *Journal of Personality and Social Psychology, 37*, 1660–1672.

Stern, L.D., Sagerser, B., Becic, E., & McBride, A. (2001, May). *Implementing the Process Dissociation Procedure with Guided Questioning.* Paper presented at the annual meeting of the Western Psychological Association, Maui, HI.

Teasdale, J.D. (1983). Negative thinking in depression: Cause, effect, or reciprocal relationship? *Advances in Behaviour Research and Therapy, 5*, 3–25.

Watkins, P.C., Grimm, D.L., May, S., Krueger, E., & Whitney, A. (2000a, June). *Impact of self-referent processing on unconscious memory bias in depression.* Paper presented at the 12th Annual Convention of the American Psychological Society, Miami Beach, FL.

Watkins, P.C., Martin, C.K., & Stern, L.D. (2000b). Unconscious memory bias in depression: Perceptual and conceptual processes. *Journal of Abnormal Psychology, 109*, 282–289.

Watkins, P.C., Mathews, A., Williamson, D.A., & Fuller, R.D. (1992). Mood-congruent memory in depression: Emotional priming or elaboration? *Journal of Abnormal Psychology, 101*, 581–586.

Watkins, P.C., Vache, K., Verney, S.P., Muller, S., & Mathews, A. (1996). Unconscious mood-congruent memory bias in depression. *Journal of Abnormal Psychology, 105*, 34–41.

Weldon, M.S., & Coyote, K.C. (1996). Failure to find the picture superiority effect in implicit conceptual memory tests. *Journal of Experimental Psychology: Learning, Memory, and Cognition, 22*, 670–686.

Whitney, A.A., Watkins, P.C., & May, S.A. (2000, April). *Themes of implicit mood-congruent memories in depression.* Presentation to the Annual Convention of the Western Psychological Association, Portland OR.

Williams, J.M.G., Watts, F.N., MacLeod, C., & Mathews, A. (1988). *Cognitive psychology and the emotional disorders.* New York: Wiley.

Williams, J.M.G., Watts, F.N., MacLeod, C., Mathews, A. (1997). *Cognitive psychology and emotional disorders; Second edition.* Chichester, UK: Wiley.

COGNITION AND EMOTION, 2002, *16* (3), 403–422

Thought suppression and memory biases during and after depressive moods

Richard M. Wenzlaff, Jo Meier, and Danette M. Salas

University of Texas at San Antonio, USA

Previous research indicates that formerly depressed individuals engage in high levels of thought suppression that can mask depressive cognitions. However, suppression may also ironically foster a vigilance for unwanted thoughts that promotes uncertainty about ambiguous information and distorts memory. The present study tested this possibility. Formerly dysphoric, currently dysphoric, and never-dysphoric participants listened to a series of statements describing life events that were positive, negative, or ambiguous. In a subsequent recognition phase, participants reviewed a series of statements and rated each for the likelihood that it had been presented earlier. The recognition list included positive and negative disambiguated versions of the original items. Compared to the never-dysphoric group, formerly dysphoric individuals were more likely to endorse negative disambiguations. As predicted, this bias was associated with higher levels of thought suppression and greater uncertainty about the meaning of ambiguous situations, suggesting an ongoing conflict between positive and negative thoughts.

Cognitive accounts of depression maintain that negative biases often persist after the mood disturbance has abated, tainting judgements and memory in ways that can undermine emotional well-being and ultimately precipitate a relapse (Sacco & Beck, 1995). Although lingering biases could help explain the high relapse rate for depression (Judd, 1997), it has proved difficult to find empirical evidence for them. Instead, research has generally found that cognitive biases ebb and flow with depressive moods, suggesting that negative thinking may simply be a by-product of the emotional disturbance (Ingram, Miranda, & Segal, 1998).

The possibility that cognitive biases are simply secondary symptoms of depressed moods calls into question the cognitive account of depression and the treatments that derive from it. However, recent research supports the cognitive

Correspondence should be addressed to Richard M. Wenzlaff, Department of Psychology, University of Texas at San Antonio, San Antonio, TX 78249-0652, USA.

E-mail: rwenzlaff@utsa.edu

This research was supported by a Faculty Grant Award to the first author from the University of Texas at San Antonio.

http://www.tandf.co.uk/journals/pp/02699931.html   DOI:10.1080/02699930143000545

view by suggesting that depressive biases do in fact persist following a depressive episode, but are difficult to detect because of thought suppression. This works indicates that formerly depressed individuals not only report high levels of chronic thought suppression, but they also show subtle signs of depressive biases when competing cognitive demands undermine mental control (Wenzlaff & Bates, 1998; Wenzlaff & Eisenberg, 2001; Wenzlaff, Rude, Taylor, Stultz, & Sweatt, 2001). These findings suggest that formerly depressed individuals are engaged in an ongoing struggle to inhibit the depressive biases that still plague them. The present study extends this research by examining the possibility that formerly dysphoric individuals' suppression efforts may promote uncertainty and distort memory for ambiguous information.

RESEARCH ON POST-DEPRESSION COGNITION

Formerly depressed individuals are at high risk of relapse, with recurrence rates as high as 80% (Judd, 1997). Thus, if cognitive biases foster the development of depression, they should be detectable in the cognitions of these at-risk individuals. In the search for a cognitive vulnerability to depression, investigators have typically compared the thought reports of at-risk individuals to those of depressed and normal groups (Blackburn, Jones, & Lewin, 1986; Dohr, Rush, & Bersnstein, 1989). Although the research confirms a high rate of negative thinking among depressed individuals, it has generally failed to find reliable evidence of a persistent cognitive bias among at-risk individuals. Contrary to the notion that negative thoughts persist beyond depression, the findings indicate that the negative thinking associated with depression abates along with the mood disturbance. In a comprehensive review of this research, Ingram et al. (1998) state that ''An inescapable conclusion from the majority of these studies is that depressive cognition is largely [mood] state dependent'' (p. 157).

Research in this area has typically relied on standardised measures of depressive thinking that ask participants to indicate their endorsement of depression-relevant attitudes, thoughts, or appraisals. Examples include the Dysfunctional Attitude Scale (DAS; Weissman & Beck, 1978), the Automatic Thoughts Questionnaire (Hollon & Kendall, 1980), and the Attributional Style Questionnaire (ASQ, Seligman, Abramson, Semmel, & von Baeyer, 1979). These methods of assessment may be insensitive to persistent depressive thinking for at least two reasons. First, the measures were originally designed to assess dysfunctional thinking among actively depressed individuals. The cognitions that persist in the aftermath of depression are likely to be less blatant than the negative thinking that accompanies an active depressive episode. After all, cognitive theory suggests that if depressive thinking were manifestly negative, the person would be in a state of depression, not remission. Thus, the negative biases that persist in the aftermath of depression are likely to be subtle and therefore difficult to detect with standard self-report measures.

Another problem with self-report measures of depressive thinking is that they invite self-censorship. The high face validity of the items can alert respondents to the positive and negative implications of their ratings. Individuals—particularly those recovering from a depressive episode—may be reluctant to endorse items that cast themselves in an unfavourable light. Indeed, recent research indicates that formerly depressed individuals frequently try to suppress negative thoughts (Beevers, Wenzlaff, Hayes, & Scott, 1999; Wenzlaff & Bates, 1998; Wenzlaff & Eisenberg, 2001).

Recognising the limitations of self-report measures, a growing number of investigators recommend the use of cognitive measures that may be more sensitive to subtle biases and less susceptible to self-report biases (Gotlib, Kurtzman, & Blehar, 1997; Hedlund & Rude, 1995; Rude, Covich, Jarrold, Hedlund, & Zenter, 2001; Segal & Dobson, 1992). However, these measures alone have not revealed post-depression biases. For example, some investigators have employed a modified version of the Stroop Test, where participants are asked to name the ink colour of depressed, manic, or neutral content targets. A depressive bias should draw attention to the depression-relevant words, resulting in slower response times to naming the ink colour. Although the findings indicate that actively depressed individuals are particularly slow to name the colours of depression-relevant words, at-risk individuals do not display these interference effects (for a review see Gotlib & Krasnoperova, 1998). Investigators have found a similar pattern of results when assessing memory. Actively depressed individuals show a bias for negative memories, but at-risk individuals do not (for reviews, see Blaney, 1980; Gotlib & Krasnoperova, 1998; Ingram et al., 1998; Matt, Vazquez, & Campbell, 1992).

In the light of these findings, investigators have speculated that depressive biases become dormant during remission but can be reactivated by negative mood states that foster associations to the latent cognitions (Miranda & Persons, 1988). Partial support for this "mood-priming hypothesis" comes from correlational studies showing that at-risk individuals display more negative thinking during naturally occurring negative mood shifts (Miranda & Persons, 1988; Miranda, Persons, & Byers, 1990; Roberts & Kassel, 1996). In addition, several studies have attempted to prime latent depressive cognitions by using mood induction procedures. With some notable exceptions (e.g., Dykman, 1997), most of these studies have shown that during transient negative mood shifts, at-risk individuals are more likely than never-depressed people to display depression-related cognitions. For example, following a negative mood induction, at-risk individuals are more likely to endorse dysfunctional attitudes than are never-depressed individuals (for a review see Ingram et al., 1998). The experimental induction of negative moods in at-risk individuals has also revealed more subtle cognitive biases in at-risk individuals, including depression-related shifts in attention and memory (for a review see Gotlib & Krasnoperova, 1998).

Recent research, however, has challenged the assumption that mood priming is necessary to facilitate the detection of post-depression biases. This research indicates that the imposition of a cognitive load (e.g., rehearsal of a series of numbers or time constraints) can reveal subtle, depressive biases in at-risk individuals without affecting mood (Wenzlaff & Bates, 1998; Wenzlaff et al., 2001; Wenzlaff & Eisenberg, 2001). The findings suggest that cognitive demands may temporarily disrupt at-risk individuals' suppression efforts, thereby allowing detection of the suppressed biases. This possibility highlights the potential importance of considering the role that mental control efforts may play in masking post-depression biases.

THE ROLE OF THOUGHT SUPPRESSION

Compared to never-depressed people, at-risk individuals report higher levels of chronic thought suppression (Beevers et al., 1999; Wenzlaff & Bates, 1998; Wenzlaff & Eisenberg, 2001; Wenzlaff et al., 2001; Wenzlaff, Rude, & West, in press) and expend more effort trying to maintain a positive frame of mind (Coyne & Calarco, 1995). This state of affairs argues against the notion of dormant biases, suggesting instead that depressive cognitions play an active role in at-risk individuals' mental lives. This possibility raises some relevant questions about the mental control process and its impact on post-depression biases.

The suppression process

The study of mental control has led to the development of *ironic process theory* (Wegner, 1994; Wegner & Wenzlaff, 1996). This theory suggests that thought suppression involves two mechanisms: an intentional distraction process that diverts attention away from unwanted thoughts; and a monitoring system that remains vigilant for intrusions that call for renewed distraction. Although the distraction process is effortful and consciously guided, the monitoring system is usually unconscious and less demanding of mental effort. Under normal circumstances, these two processes work in concert so that the distraction process diverts awareness from undesirable thoughts and the monitoring system subtly prompts it to further action at the first sign of failure. At one level, then, the distraction and monitoring processes are complementary, helping assure that unwanted thoughts are relegated to the fringes of consciousness. At another level, however, the monitoring system can undermine the goal of suppression by maintaining vigilance for the very thoughts that have been targeted for elimination. In this sense, the monitoring process helps assure that the unwanted thoughts never become dormant. According to this model, the monitoring process should be most likely to usher unwanted thoughts into awareness when distraction is either voluntarily relinquished or disabled by competing cognitive demands. Indeed, numerous laboratory studies have demonstrated a surge in target thoughts under these conditions (for a review, see Wenzlaff & Wegner, 2000).

Suppression and post-depression cognition

Although there is considerable support for ironic processes theory, its relevance to depression risk has only recently been examined. In the first study that tested the possibility that suppression can mask depressive biases, Wenzlaff and Bates (1998) found that the addition of a cognitive load (rehearsal of a series of numbers) caused a depressive shift in at risk individuals' performance on an experimental task. The task involved rearranging five words contained in sets of six scrambled words (e.g., "future the dismal very bright looks") to form sentences (e.g., "the future looks very bright" or "the future looks very dismal"). Under no-load conditions, the at-risk and never-depressed groups equally favoured positive sentences, whereas the depressed group was more likely to produce negative themes. However, the imposition of a cognitive load caused at-risk individuals to shift toward negative statements, making their responses resemble those of the depressed group. This effect was significantly correlated with a measure of chronic thought suppression.

In a follow-up study, Wenzlaff, Rude, and Taylor (2001) assessed formerly depressed individuals' performance on a novel measure of thought accessibility that involved detecting emotionally relevant words in a letter grid. The results indicated that under normal circumstances both the at-risk and control groups identified mostly positive words. However, under cognitive load, the at-risk group identified more negative words, reaching levels equivalent to an actively depressed group. A similar pattern of findings was obtained in a study where participants interpreted homophones under varying time constraints (Wenzlaff & Eisenberg, 2001). Unlike never-depressed participants, formerly depressed individuals interpreted recorded homophones in a more negative fashion when they were under time pressure.

In each of these studies, the load-related surge in negative thinking was significantly correlated with measures of chronic thought suppression. Moreover, each of the studies employed tasks that involved ambiguous information (e.g., identifying positive or negative solutions to scrambled sentences, homophones, or words imbedded in a letter grid). In these types of ambiguous situations, at-risk individuals normally favoured the positive alternatives, but demonstrated a negative shift when cognitive demands arose. Because cognitive demands are more apt to interfere with controlled processes rather than automatic ones (Posner & Snyder, 1975; Shiffrin & Schneider, 1977), the load-induced shift suggests that, despite their desire to maintain a positive frame of mind, at-risk individuals are predisposed to construe ambiguous situations in a negative manner.

The preliminary studies on suppression and post-depression cognition suggest that ambiguous information poses a special challenge for at-risk individuals. Although their initial appraisals tend to be negative, they endeavour to suppress this tendency by directing attention to more positive interpretations. At-risk individuals' conflict between their automatic negative biases and the desire to maintain a positive frame of mind should make them relatively uncertain about the meaning of ambiguous information and affect their memory for it. When evaluating ambiguous information, at-risk individuals may seek to suppress their negative tendencies by diverting attention to more benign interpretations. In the absence of added cognitive demands that could undermine suppression, at-risk individuals should produce appraisals that are indistinguishable from those of people with no history of depression. However, suppression also helps assure a lingering awareness of the unwanted thoughts that could foster uncertainty. Thus, even though at-risk individuals may report benign appraisals of ambiguous information, they should be more uncertain of their evaluations than should people with no history of depression.

In addition to fostering doubts about their appraisals of ambiguous information, the suppression-related monitoring process should also influence at-risk individuals' memory for the material. The monitoring process should enhance the accessible of negative interpretations, thereby tainting at-risk individuals' memory for ambiguous information. Thus, compared to people with no history of depression, at-risk individuals should be more likely to endorse negative interpretations of the ambiguous information on a subsequent recognition task. Moreover, their level of endorsement should be directly related to their levels of chronic thought suppression.

OVERVIEW

The experiment employed a task that borrowed some procedural aspects from previous research on interpretative biases in anxiety (Eysenck, Mogg, May, Richards, & Mathews, 1991). Dysphoric, at-risk, and never-dysphoric participants listened to a series of statements describing life events that had either emotionally positive, negative, or ambiguous implications. During the recordings, participants rated the positivity of each statement and their confidence about those ratings. In a subsequent recognition phase, participants reviewed a series of statements and rated each for the likelihood that it had been presented earlier. The recognition list included some items from the original list, some new, and some that involved revisions of the original ambiguous items to make them have either positive or negative connotations. Following the recognition task, participants completed a measure of chronic thought suppression. We predicted that at-risk individuals would be relatively uncertain about their positivity ratings for the ambiguous items, and they would be especially likely to endorse negative disambiguations during the recognition phase. We also predicted that these effects would be associated with high levels of chronic thought suppression.

METHOD

Participants

A total of 324 undergraduate students in introductory psychology classes at the University of Texas at San Antonio participated as an optional way of fulfilling the requirements of the course. We used the short form of the Beck Depression Inventory (BDI-SF; Beck & Beck, 1972) to determine current depression status. The BDI-SF contains 13 items and has been found to correlate .96 with the 21-item Beck Depression Inventory (Beck & Beamesderfer, 1974). Beck and Beamesderfer (1974) advised that scores below 4 indicate minimal or no depression and recommended that 8 be used as a cut-off score for moderate depression. On the basis of these criteria, we classified participants with BDI-SF scores of 0–3 as nondysphoric and those with scores of 8 and above as dysphoric.

We used the Inventory to Diagnose Depression Lifetime Version (IDD-L; Zimmerman & Coryell, 1987) to assess prior depressive moods. The IDD-L is a 22-item self-report inventory that assesses the extent and duration of previous depressive symptomatology. Total scores can range from 0 to 88. The IDD-L compares well in terms of sensitivity and specificity to the Diagnostic Interview Schedule (Zimmerman & Coryell, 1987). It also has good discriminant validity (Sakado, Sata, Uehara, Sato, & Kameda, 1996) and test-retest reliability (Sato et al., 1996). However, there is currently no established standard for defining previous depression using the IDD-L. Prior depression has sometimes been defined in terms of the presence of certain key symptoms (Roberts, Gilboa, & Gotlib, 1998), whereas in other cases the IDD-L has been used as a continuous measure with high scores indicative of prior depression (Roberts & Gotlib, 1997). To help assure validity, we chose a conservative classification approach that combined these different approaches (Wenzlaff et al., 2001; Wenzlaff et al., in press).

We determined previous depression based on three considerations: (1) Following criteria outlined in the *Diagnostic and statistical manual of mental disorders* (4th ed., DSM-IV; American Psychiatric Association, 1994), individuals had to endorse at least five different types of symptoms including either depressed mood or anhedonia (endorsement was defined as a rating of at least 2 on a scale ranging from 0 to 4 for an item describing the symptom). (2) Each symptom had to have been present for more than 2 weeks. (3) The total IDD-L score had to equal or exceed 40. The cut score of 40 was suggested by research showing an average IDD-L score of 41 for individuals identified as having previous depression on the basis of structured diagnostic interviews (Solomon, Haaga, Brody, Kirk, & Friedman, 1998).

We classified participants who scored 3 or below on the BDI-SF and met the criteria for a previous depressive episode as "at risk". Although these individuals were currently nondysphoric, their depressive history put them at a high risk for relapse. We labelled individuals as "never dysphoric" if their BDI-SF scores were 3 or below and their IDD-L scores were below 20, indicating no significant depressive history (Roberts & Gotlib, 1997; Wenzlaff & Eisenberg, 2001). Finally, we classified participants as "dysphoric" if their BDI-SF scores were 8 or above.

These criteria resulted in the classification of 72 individuals as never dysphoric, 19 as at risk, and 74 as dysphoric. The final sample consisted of 105 females and 60 males with a mean age of 21.39.

Stimulus sentences

We developed a set of sentences that could convey either a positive meaning (e.g., "My prospects for the future look very good), a negative meaning (e.g., "In the past week, nothing seems to have gone right for me"), or were ambiguous ("After the ceremony, I thought about my future"). In addition, for each of the ambiguous sentences we created a positive disambiguation (e.g., "After the ceremony, I thought about my bright future") and a negative disambiguation (e.g., "After the ceremony, I thought about my dismal future"). We pilot tested a total of 235 items (35 positive, 35 negative, 55 ambiguous, 55 positive disambiguations, and 55 negative disambiguations).

For the pilot test we created five random orders of the 230 sentences and administered them to 92 undergraduate students in introductory psychology classes at the University of Texas at San Antonio. The students participated as an optional way of fulfilling the requirements of the course. Participants rated each statement for its emotional meaning using a 7-point scale with 1 indicating "very negative" and 7 indicating "very positive". Participants also completed the BDI-SF.

To be included in the primary study, the mean rating for each positive item had to be greater than or equal to 5 and the mean score for each negative item had to be less than or equal to 3. Each ambiguous item had to meet three criteria: (1) a mean rating between 3.5 and 4.5; (2) the rating for the positive alternative had to greater than or equal to 5, and (3) the mean for the negative alternative had to be less than or equal to 3. Based on these criteria we identified a pool of 70 sentences consisting of 21 positive sentences ($M = 5.90$), 21 negative sentences ($M = 2.32$), and 28 ambiguous sentences ($M = 4.06$) with the corresponding positive and negative disambiguations ($Ms = 5.86$ and 2.40, respectively). To help ensure that the ratings of the selected items did not vary as a function of mood state, we correlated the ratings for each type of sentence type with participants' BDI-SF scores. None of the Pearson correlation coefficients exceeded .11, $ps > .30$. Table 1 shows a sample of the sentences from the final set of stimulus items.

TABLE 1
Sample stimulus items

Ambiguous sentences with positive and negative disambiguations in parentheses
    I could sense the (positive/negative) mood of the group.
    Last night my friend commented on my (cheery/tired) appearance.
    My doctor called to discuss the (good/bad) results of my test.
    The photo album brought many (happy/sad) memories to mind.
    The experience made me think about my (fortunate/unfortunate) situation.

Negative sentences
    Their comments made me think that people don't really know me.
    I have been worried about my well-being lately.
    I turned down a chance to go out because I was in a bad mood.
    I often wonder if I will ever please my family.
    People seem to expect too much of me.

Positive sentences
    I was encouraged by the news.
    My prospects for the future look very good.
    My life is usually pretty interesting.
    In general, I feel like I'm on the right track.
    I met a new person and we really hit it off.

Procedure

Participants assembled for the experiment in groups of 20 to 30. The experimenter indicated that the first part of the study was concerned with their perceptions of various life experiences. They were to listen to an audiorecording of a series of first-person statements about life experiences. The experimenter told participants to try to personally identify with each statement and then to make two ratings after hearing each. Using 7-point scales, participants rated the positivity of each statement (1 = very negative, 7 = very positive) and their level of certainty about each positivity rating (1 = not at all certain, 7 = very certain).

The audiorecording presented each sentence followed by a delay of 4 seconds to allow participants to make their ratings. We created 5 versions of the audiorecorded sentences. Each recording consisted of 21 ambiguous items, 14 positive items, and 14 negative items randomly selected from the pool of 70 pretested items. The ordering of the statements for each recording was randomly determined. We used each of the 5 sets of recordings in sequential order corresponding to the temporal order of the experimental sessions. Thus, session 1 was assigned recording 1, session 2 recording 2, and so on, with the pattern repeating itself (e.g., session 6 was assigned recording 1, session 7 recording 2, etc.). After the recording, participants worked for 5 min on a task involving anagrams that was billed as a measure of linguistic preferences. The actual purpose of the anagram task was to allow for the passage of time to minimise recency effects during the subsequent recognition phase. Participants were then presented with a list of statements and were told that some of the items were on the original list and some were not. For each statement they rated the likelihood that it had been presented earlier by using a 7-point scale (1 = definitely not on the original list, 7 = definitely on the original list).

The recognition list consisted of 56 statements involving three categories. The first category contained 21 "old items", equally distributed among the previously presented positive, negative, and ambiguous statements. These items were randomly selected from the presentation list. The second category consisted of 21 "new items" equally distributed among positive, negative, and ambiguous statements from the pretested pool that had not been included in the presentation phase. The third category involved 14 "disambiguated items", consisting of 7 positive and 7 negative versions of the items that were originally presented in an ambiguous form and not included among the "old items". We used a random procedure to determine whether the item was disambiguated to convey a positive or negative meaning. There were 5 versions of the recognition list that coincided with the 5 versions of the presentation list. The order of the statements for each recognition list was randomly determined.

After making their recognition ratings, participants completed the BDI-SF and the IDD-L (described earlier). Finally, participants reported their thought suppression practices using the 15-item White Bear Suppression Inventory (WBSI; Wegner & Zanakos, 1994). The WBSI assesses chronic thought suppression tendencies by asking people to rate their endorsement of suppression-relevant practices (e.g., "I always try to put problems out of my mind") using a 5-point scale (strongly agree–strongly disagree). It shows good internal and temporal reliability as well as concurrent validity (Muris & Merckelbach, 1997; Muris, Merckelbach, & Horselenberg, 1996; van den Hout, Merckelbach, & Pool, 1996; Wegner & Zanakos, 1994).

RESULTS

Manipulation check

To ensure that the positive, negative, and ambiguous items were perceived accordingly, we entered the 7-point positivity ratings into a 3×3 ANOVA with dysphoric status (never dysphoric/at risk/dysphoric) as a between-subjects factor and item type (negative/positive/ambiguous) as a within-subject factor. The results indicated a reliable main effect for item type, $F(2, 161) = 1,949.68$, $p < .01$. The ANOVA did not indicate any other reliable effects, $ps > .10$. Further analysis of the main effect for item type indicated that—as intended—the positive items were rated more positively ($M = 5.83$) than were either the ambiguous items ($M = 4.14$), $t(164) = 30.27$, $p < .01$, or the negative items ($M = 2.31$). In turn, the negative items were judged more negatively than the ambiguous items, $t(164) = 34.25$, $p < .01$.

Recognition ratings for disambiguated items

We analysed the 7-point recognition ratings for the disambiguated items using a 3 × 2 ANOVA with dysphoric status (never dysphoric/at risk/dysphoric) as a between-subjects factor and item type (negative disambiguation/positive disambiguation) as a within-subject factor. The results indicated a reliable interaction, $F(2, 162) = 25.66$, $p < .01$. There were no lower order effects, $ps > .10$.

As shown in Table 2, both the at-risk and dysphoric groups judged the negative disambiguated items as more likely to have been on the original list than did the never-dysphoric group. There was no reliable difference in the ratings of the negative disambiguated items between the at-risk and dysphoric groups. In contrast, both the at-risk and dysphoric groups gave lower endorsements for the positive disambiguations than did the never-dysphoric group. It is worth noting, however, that the group differences are relative—none of the groups strongly endorsed the negative or positive disambiguations.

Within-group comparisons indicated that both the at-risk and dysphoric groups gave higher endorsements for the negative disambiguated items than they did for the positive disambiguations, $t(18) = 2.21$, $p < .05$ and $t(73) = 5.09$, $p < .01$, respectively. Conversely, the never-dysphoric group endorsed positive disambiguations at a higher rate than they did the negative disambiguated items, $t(71) = 4.59$, $p < .05$.

Recognition ratings for original and new items

We examined the recognition ratings for the original and new items using a 3 × 3 × 2 ANOVA with dysphoric status (never dysphoric/at risk/dysphoric) as a between-subjects factor, and item type (ambiguous/negative/positive) and

TABLE 2
Recognition ratings as a function of dysphoric status

Item type	Never dysphoric (n = 72)		At risk (n = 19)		Dysphoric (n = 74)	
	M	(SD)	M	(SD)	M	(SD)
Negative disambiguation	2.17$_a$	(1.14)	2.83$_b$	(1.12)	3.09$_b$	(1.27)
Positive disambiguation	2.99$_a$	(1.25)	2.24$_b$	(0.74)	2.17$_b$	(0.88)
Old ambiguous	5.90$_a$	(1.26)	5.95$_a$	(0.80)	6.02$_a$	(1.09)
New ambiguous	2.18$_a$	(0.71)	2.30$_a$	(0.79)	2.40$_a$	(0.89)
Old negative	5.90$_a$	(1.01)	5.99$_a$	(0.70)	6.37$_b$	(0.67)
New negative	1.90$_a$	(0.80)	1.86$_a$	(0.69)	2.00$_a$	(0.75)
Old positive	6.23$_a$	(0.86)	6.36$_a$	(0.70)	6.28$_a$	(0.92)
New positive	1.96$_a$	(0.91)	1.92$_a$	(1.46)	1.80$_a$	(0.91)

Note: Means could range from 1 to 7. Higher scores indicate greater recognition. Means in the same row that do not share a common subscript differ at $p < .05$.

familiarity (old/new) as within-subject factors. A breakdown of the means and the simple effects tests are shown in Table 2. The ANOVA revealed a reliable main effect for familiarity, $F(1, 162) = 1,912.88$, $p < .01$, indicating that old items received higher recognition ratings ($M = 6.12$) than did new items ($M = 2.04$). There was also a reliable interaction between familiarity and item type, $F(2, 161) = 10.95$, $p < .01$. Old ambiguous items received lower endorsements ($M = 5.96$) than did either old positive ($M = 6.27$) or old negative items ($M = 6.12$), $t(164) = 3.91$, $p < .01$ and $t(164) = 1.93$, $p = .05$, respectively. In contrast, new ambiguous items received higher endorsements ($M = 2.29$) than did either new positive ($M = 1.89$) or new negative ($M = 1.94$), $t(164) = 3.96$, $p < .01$ and $t(164) = 3.99$, $p < .01$, respectively. This pattern suggests that participants found it more difficult to distinguish between the old and new ambiguous items than between old and new positive or negative items.

The main analysis also revealed a marginal interaction between dysphoric status and item type, $F(4, 324) = 2.09$, $p = .08$. Further analyses indicated there were no reliable group differences for the ambiguous and positive items, $F(2, 162) = 1.07$, n.s. and $F < 1$, respectively. However, the negative items did reliably vary as a function of dysphoric status, $F(2, 162) = 5.48$, $p < .01$. Additional analyses indicated that the dysphoric group gave higher endorsements for the negative items ($M = 4.19$) than did either the never-dysphoric group ($M = 3.90$) or the at-risk group ($M = 3.92$), $t(144) = 3.15$, $p < .01$ and $t(91) = 2.16$, $p < .05$, respectively.

The absence of a three-way interaction, $F < 1$, suggests that the dysphoric group's relatively high endorsement of negative items may reflect a negative response bias rather than a memory bias *per se*. However, an examination of the simple effects tests shown in Table 2 suggests that the dysphoric group's relatively high endorsement of negative items is primarily attributable to the old negative items, rather than the new. An ANOVA with dysphoric status as a between-subjects factor indicated reliable group differences for the old negative items, $F(2, 162) = 5.96$, $p < .01$. As shown in Table 2, the dysphoric group endorsed old negative items at a higher rate ($M = 6.37$) than did either the never-dysphoric or the at-risk groups. However, the new negative items did not reliably vary as a function of dysphoric status, $F < 1$. Thus, although we cannot rule out the possibility of a negative response bias among the dysphoric group, this account is weakened by the lack of group differences for the new negative items.

Certainty Ratings

To test our prediction that the at-risk group would be relatively uncertain of their positivity ratings for the ambiguous items, we entered the certainty ratings into a 3×3 ANOVA with dysphoric status (never dysphoric/at risk/dysphoric) as a between-subjects factor, and sentence type (ambiguous/negative/positive) as a within-subject factor. The results indicated a reliable main effect for sentence type, $F(2, 161) = 292.00$, $p < .01$. Further analysis of this main effect indicated lower certainty ratings for the ambiguous items ($M = 3.49$) than for the positive items ($M = 5.87$) which, in turn, were lower than the negative items ($M = 6.02$), $t(164) = 23.02$, $p < .01$ and $t(164) = 3.44$, $p < .01$, respectively. However, the ANOVA also revealed a reliable interaction between dysphoric status and sentence type, $F(4, 324) = 9.54$, $p < .01$ (see Table 3).

Analysis of the interaction revealed no reliable differences among the groups for either the negative or the positive items, $p > .25$. However, the certainty ratings for the ambiguous items did reliably vary as a function of dysphoric status, $F(2, 162) = 26.15$, $p < .01$. As shown in Table 3, both the at-risk and dysphoric groups indicated more uncertainty about the positivity of the ambiguous items than did the never dysphoric group. There were no reliable differences among the at-risk and dysphoric group.

We predicted that at-risk individuals' relative uncertainty about the ambiguous items would be related to their tendency to endorse negative disambiguations. Indeed, the more uncertain at-risk individuals were about the positivity of the ambiguous items, the more likely they were to endorse the negative disambiguations, $r(17) = .54$, $p < .01$. There was no comparable correlation for the never-dysphoric group, $r(70) = .03$, n.s. There was a relationship between uncertainty and endorsement of the negative disambiguated items for the dysphoric group, $r(72) = .46$, $p < .01$. However, there was also a strong correlation for the dysphoric group between dysphoria level (as measured by the BDI-SF), and endorsement of the negative disambiguations, $r(72) = .57$, $p < .01$. After controlling for BDI-SF scores, the correlation between certainty and negative disambiguations was nonsignificant for the dysphoric group, $r(71) = .16$, n.s..

TABLE 3

Mean certainty ratings for ambiguous items and mean suppression scores

Type of rating	Never dysphoric	At risk	Dysphoric
Certainty			
M	4.18_a	3.06_b	2.94_b
(SD)	(1.30)	(1.02)	(0.80)
Suppression			
M	2.95_a	3.61_b	3.93_c
(SD)	(0.72)	(0.68)	(0.55)

Note. Certainty scores could range from 1 to 7 and suppression scores could range from 1 to 5. Higher scores indicate either greater certainty or more chronic thought suppression. Means in the same row that do not share a subscript differ at $p < .05$.

Thought suppression

We predicted that at-risk individuals would be especially likely to engage in thought suppression, and that reliance on this type of mental control would be positively correlated with both uncertainty about the ambiguous items and the tendency to endorse negative disambiguations. To test these predictions, we first examined the suppression ratings using an ANOVA with dysphoric status (never dysphoric/at risk/dysphoric) as the factor. This analysis indicated that the suppression ratings varied as a function of dysphoric status, $F(2, 162) = 43.31$, $p < .01$. As shown in Table 3, the at-risk group reported higher levels of chronic thought suppression than did the never-dysphoric group. The dysphoric group reported the highest levels of suppression.

For each of the groups, we computed a Pearson correlation between the suppression scores and the certainty ratings for the ambiguous items. The resulting correlation for the never-dysphoric group was nonsignificant, $r(70) = .15$, n.s. However, as predicted, higher levels of thought suppression among at-risk individuals were associated with greater uncertainty about the positivity of the ambiguous items, $r(17) = .74$, $p < .01$. There was also a reliable, positive correlation between at-risk individuals' suppression scores and their endorsement of the negative disambiguated items, $r(17) = .62$, $p < .01$.

Analysis of the dysphoric group also revealed a positive correlation between levels of thought suppression and uncertainty about the positivity of the ambiguous items, $r(72) = .54$, $p < .01$. In addition, the suppression scores of the dysphoric group were positively associated with endorsement of the negative disambiguations, $r(72) = .39$, $p < .01$. However, after controlling for levels of dysphoria, this correlation was nonsignificant, $r(71) = .11$, n.s.

DISCUSSION

Compared to the dysphoric group, both the at-risk and never-dysphoric groups produced similar recognition ratings for the original set of negative items. This finding is reminiscent of previous research that has failed to find differences on cognitive measures between at-risk and never-depressed individuals. However, these groups did differ with respect to their ratings for the negative and positive disambiguations. Both the at-risk and dysphoric groups reported higher recognition for the negative disambiguated items than did the never-dysphoric group. In contrast, the never-dysphoric group endorsed positive disambiguations at a higher rate than did either the at-risk or dysphoric groups. These findings indicate a negative bias among both at-risk and dysphoric individuals, and a positive bias for the never-dysphoric group (for a review of self-enhancing biases see Taylor & Brown, 1988). Also, as predicted, at-risk individuals were more uncertain of the original assessments of the positivity of the negative disambiguations than were the other groups. This uncertainty was related to high levels of thought suppression and was positively correlated with at-risk individuals' tendency to endorse negative disambiguations.

Taken together, the findings provide support for the idea that at-risk individuals possess a depressive bias that is usually masked by thought suppression. Although suppression can inhibit the influence of depressive biases, it can also perpetuate them by fostering vigilance for unwanted thoughts. When confronted with ambiguous information, at-risk individuals may try to suppress the negative interpretations that are made salient by their underlying biases. The ironic nature of suppression helps assure the lingering influence of unwanted thoughts, thus fostering uncertainty about the meaning of ambiguous information and tainting memory for it. Although the present study provides support for the suppression hypothesis, there are also methodological and theoretical issues that deserve attention.

Methodological and conceptual Issues

Although previous research using free recall has often found evidence of mood-congruent memory among actively depressed individuals (for reviews see Blaney, 1980; Matt Vazquez, & Campbell, 1992), it has typically failed to detect this bias for recognition memory (Deijen, Orlebeke, & Rijsdijk, 1994; Neshat-Doost, Taghavi, Moradi, Yule, & Dalgleish, 1998; Zuroff, Colussy, & Wielgus, 1983; but see Dunbar & Lishman, 1984). In contrast, the present study found evidence of a recognition bias among actively dysphoric individuals for both the original negative items and the negative disambiguations. Differences in methodology between the present study and previous research may account for the unusual finding of a recognition bias among dysphoric individuals. Unlike previous research that has typically tested memory for positive or negative adjectives (Ceply & Tyson, 1988; Neshat-Doost et al., 1998; Zuroff et al., 1983) the present study used statements describing life experiences relevant to depression. Compared to adjective lists, the greater complexity and potential self-relevance of the statements may have made them more sensitive to mood-relevant biases. In addition, the recognition task involved interval ratings that may have enhanced detection of subtle biases.

Another issue that warrants consideration involves the relevance of the present findings to clinical depression. Some investigators have questioned whether findings from studies using self-reported depression among college students can be generalised to clinically depressed patients (Gotlib, 1984; Hammen, 1980; Kendall, Hollon, Beck, Hammen, & Ingram, 1987). Others have claimed that this type of research often provides useful insights into clinical phenomena (Vredenburg, Flett, & Krames, 1993; Weary, Edwards, & Jacobson, 1995). The ongoing debate centres on issues of severity, stability, and specificity of symptoms, demographics, and larger questions concerning categorical and dimensional systems of classification. Notwithstanding the complicated nature of these issues, one relatively straightforward way to address the question of clinical relevance, is to compare the findings of studies with depressed patients to those using dysphoric college students.

Vredenburg et al. (1993) reviewed studies with dysphoric college students in relation to research with depressed patients, and found that the two approaches generally yielded comparable results. This conclusion was based on studies examining attribution style, locus of control, social aspects of depression, and personality factors related to achievement. Comparable results with college and clinical samples have also been obtained in depression research examining self-verification processes (Swann, Wenzlaff, Krull, & Pelham, 1992; Giesler, Josephs, & Swann, 1996), attitudes (Eaves & Rush, 1984; Weissman, 1979), attentional biases (Gotlib & McCann, 1984; Klieger & Cordner, 1990), and thoughts (Hollon & Kendall, 1980; Krantz & Hammen, 1979). Thus, there is a substantial body of research that indicates a meaningful correspondence between the depression-related effects obtained with clinical and nonclinical samples. Although this fact helps bolster the relevance of the present research, it is not a substitute for research with a clinical sample. Until such evidence is obtained, clinical generalisations from the present study remain tentative.

Methodological constraints also raise an important question concerning the role of thought suppression in the obtained results. Although our measure of chronic suppression (i.e., the WBSI) indicated especially high rates for the at-risk group, it is possible that there were temporal and situational variations in their level of suppression during the experiment. The problem, of course, is that it is not possible to observe directly the mental processes in question. Thus, we cannot draw firm conclusions about the role thought suppression played in at-risk participants' judgements and memory. Nevertheless, the suppression hypothesis is bolstered by results that are consistent with the model and compatible with existing research on mental control.

The issue of vulnerability

Research reported elsewhere in this issue by Rude, Wenzlaff, Gibbs, Vane, and Whitney, indicates that thought suppression is associated with an increased risk of developing depression. This finding is consistent with previous research showing that suppression can ironically make unwanted thoughts more accessible, thereby undermining mood (Wenzlaff & Wegner, 2000). In the present study, at-risk individuals' efforts to suppress unfavourable interpretations of ambiguous situations may have made the negative implications more salient, thereby tainting memory of the experience. In everyday life, this state of affairs could foster distorted memories for ambiguous situations. If the person were to experience added life stress (e.g., a personal loss, a setback, or increased demands), it could deplete the cognitive resources necessary for distraction and result in a surge of unwanted thoughts that could foster a descent into depression. Once the depressive mood has taken hold, the negative emotional state itself could further deplete cognitive resources needed for effective distraction (Hartlage, Alloy, Vazquez, & Dykman, 1993). The depressive mood may further undermine suppression by leading the individual to select negative distracters that eventually serve as reminders of the unwanted thoughts (Wenzlaff, Wegner, & Roper, 1988). Although this scenario is speculative, it is consistent with a growing body of research linking thought suppression, negative thoughts, and vulnerability to depression.

Manuscript received 15 October 2000
Revised manuscript received 19 April 2000

REFERENCES

American Psychiatric Association. (1994). *Diagnostic and statistical manual of mental disorders* (4th ed.). Washington, DC: Author.

Beck, A., & Beamesderfer, A. (1974). Assessment of depression: The depression inventory. In P. Pichot (Ed.), *Psychological measurements in psychopharmacology. Modern problems in Pharmacopsychiatry* (Vol. 7, pp. 151–169). Basel, Darger.

Beck, A., & Beck, R. (1972). Screening depressed patients in family practice: A rapid technic. *Postgraduate Medicine, 52*, 81–85.

Beevers, C.G., Wenzlaff, R.M., Hayes, A.M., Scott, W.D. (1999). Depression and the ironic effects of thought suppression. *Clinical Psychology: Science and Practice, 6*, 133–148.

Blackburn, I.M., Jones, S., & Lewin, R.J.P. (1986). Cognitive style in depression. *British Journal of Clinical Psychology, 25*, 241–251.

Blaney, P.H. (1980). Affect and memory: A review. *Psychological Bulletin, 99*, 229–246.

Ceply, E., & Tyson, P.D. (1988). Memory deficits in psychiatric outpatients and affective ratings of positive and neutral lists of words. *Perceptual and Motor Skills, 66*, 255–263.

Coyne, J.C., & Calarco, M.M. (1995). Effects of the experience of depression: Application of focus groups and survey methodologies. *Psychiatry, 58*, 149–163.

Deijen, J.B., Orlebeke, J.F., Rijsdijk, F.V. (1994). Effect of depression on psychomotor skills, eye movements and recognition memory. *Journal of Affective Disorders, 29*, 33–40.

Dohr, K.B., Rush, A.J., & Bernstein, I.H. (1989). Cognitive biases in depression. *Journal of Abnormal Psychology, 98*, 263–267.

Dunbar, G.C., & Lishman, W.A. (1984). Depression, recognition-memory and hedonic tone: A signal detection analysis. *British Journal of Psychiatry, 144*, 376–382.

Dykman, B.M. (1997). A test of whether negative emotional priming facilitates access to latent dysfunctional attitudes. *Cognition and Emotion, 11*, 197–222.

Eaves, G., & Rush, A.J. (1984). Cognitive patterns in symptomatic and remitted unipolar major depression. *Journal of Abnormal Psychology, 93*, 31–40.

Eysenck, M.W., Mogg, K., May, J., Richards, A., & Mathews, A. (1991). Bias in interpretation of ambiguous sentences related to threat in anxiety. *Journal of Abnormal Psychology, 100*, 144–150.

Giesler, R.B., Josephs, R.A., & Swann, W.B. (1996). Self-verification in clinical depression: The desire for negative evaluation. *Journal of Abnormal Psychology, 105*, 358–368.

Gotlib, I.H. (1984). Depression and general psychopathology in university students. *Journal of Abnormal Psychology, 93*, 19–30.

Gotlib, I.H., & Krasnoperova, E. (1998). Biased information processing as a vulnerability factor for depression. *Behavior Therapy, 29*, 603–617.

Gotlib, I.H., Kurtzman, H.S., & Blehar, M.C. (1997). Cognition and depression: Issues and future directions. *Cognition and Emotion, 11*, 663–673.

Gotlib, I.H., & McCann, C.D. (1984). Construct accessibility and clinical depression: A longitudinal investigation. *Journal of Abnormal Psychology, 96*, 199–204.

Gross, J.J. (1998). The emerging field of emotion regulation: An integrative review. *Review of General Psychology, 2*, 271–299.

Hammen, C.L. (1980). Depression in college students: Beyond the Beck Depression Inventory. *Journal of Consulting and Clinical Psychology, 48*, 126–128.

Hartlage, S., Alloy, L.B., Vazquez, C., & Dykman, B. (1993). Automatic and effortful processing in depression. *Psychological Bulletin, 113*, 247–278.

Hedlund, S., & Rude, S.S. (1995). Evidence of latent depressive schemas in formerly depressed individuals. *Journal of Abnormal Psychology, 104*, 517–525.

Hollon, S.D., & Kendall, P.C. (1980). Cognitive self-statements in depression: Development of an automatic thoughts questionnaire. *Cognitive Therapy and Research, 4*, 383–395.

Ingram, R.E., Miranda, J., & Segal, Z.V. (1998). *Cognitive vulnerability to depression*. New York: Guilford Press.

Judd, L.L. (1997). The clinical course of unipolar major depressive disorders. *Archives of General Psychiatry, 54*, 989–991.

Kendall, P.C., Hollon, S.D., Beck, A.T., Hammen, C.L., & Ingram, R.E. (1987). Issues and recommendations regarding use of the Beck Depression Inventory. *Journal of Abnormal Psychology, 11*, 289–299.

Klieger, D.M., & Cordner, M.D. (1990). The Stroop task as measure of construct accessibility in depression. *Personality and Individual Differences, 11*, 19–27.

Krantz, S., & Hammen, C. (1979). Assessment of cognitive bias in depression. *Journal of Abnormal Psychology, 88*, 611–619.

Matt, G.E., Vazquez, C., & Campbell, W.K. (1992). Mood-congruent recall of affectively toned stimuli: A meta-analytic review. *Clinical Psychology Review, 12*, 227–255.

Miranda, J., & Persons, J.B. (1988). Dysfunctional attitudes are mood-state dependent. *Journal of Abnormal Psychology, 97*, 76–79.

Miranda, J., Persons, J.B., & Byers, C.N. (1990). Endorsement of dysfunctional beliefs depends on current mood state. *Journal of Abnormal Psychology, 99*, 237–241.

Muris, P., & Merckelbach, H. (1997). Suppression and dissociation. *Personality and Individual Differences, 23*, 523–525.

Muris, P., Merckelbach, H., & Horselenberg, R. (1996). Individual differences in thought suppression. The White Bear Suppression Inventory: Factor structure, reliability, validity and correlates. *Behaviour Research and Therapy, 34*, 501–513.

Neshat-Doost, H., Taghavi, M.R., Moradi, A.R., Yule, W., Dalgleish, T. (1998). memory for emotional trait adjectives in clinically depressed youth. *Journal of Abnormal Psychology, 107*, 642–650.

Posner, M.I., & Snyder, C.R.R. (1975). Attention and cognitive control. In R.L. Solso (Ed.), *Information processing and cognition: The Loyola symposium* (pp. 55–85). Hillsdale, NJ: Erlbaum.

Roberts, J.E., Gilboa, E., & Gotlib, I.H. (1998). Ruminative response style and vulnerability to episodes of dysphoria: Gender, neuroticism, and episode duration. *Cognitive Therapy and Research, 22*, 401–423.

Roberts, J.E., & Gotlib, I.H. (1997). Temporal variability in global self-esteem and specific self-evaluation as prospective predictors of emotional distress: Specificity in predictors and outcome. *Journal of Abnormal Psychology, 106*, 521–529.

Roberts, J.E., & Kassel, J.D. (1996). Mood-state dependence in cognitive vulnerability to depression: The roles of positive and negative affect. *Cognitive Therapy and Research, 20*, 1–12.

Rude, S.S., Covich, J., Jarrold, W., Hedlund, S., & Zentner, M. (2001). Detecting depressive schemata in vulnerability individuals: Questionnaires vs laboratory tasks. *Cognitive Therapy and Research, 25*, 103–116.

Rude, S.S., Wenzlaff, R.M., Gibbs, B., Vane, J., & Whitney, T. (this issue). Negative processing biases predict subsequent depressive symptoms. *Cognition and Emotion, 16*(3), 423–440.

Sacco, W.P., & Beck, A.T. (1995). Cognitive theory and therapy. In E.E. Beckham & W.R. Leber (Eds.), *Handbook of depression* (pp. 329–351). New York: Guilford Press.

Sakado, K., Sato, T., Uehara, T., Sato, S., & Kameda, K. (1996). Discrminant validity of the Inventory to Diagnose Depression, Lifetime Version. *Acta Psychiatrica Scandinavica, 93*, 257–260.

Sato, T., Uehara, T., Sakado, K., Sato, S., Nishioka, K., & Kasahara, Y. (1996). The test-retest reliability of the Inventory to Diagnose Depression, Lifetime Version. *Psychopathology, 29*, 154–158.

Segal, Z.V., & Dobson, K.S. (1992). Cognitive models of depression: Report from a consensus development conference. *Psychological Inquiry, 3*, 219–224.

Seligman, M.E.P., Abramson, L., Semmel, A., & von Baeyer, C. (1979). Depressive attributional style. *Journal of Abnormal Psychology, 88*, 242–248.

Shiffrin, R.M., & Schneider, W. (1977). Controlled and automatic human information processing: II. Perceptual learning, automatic attending, and a general theory. *Psychological Review, 84*, 127–190.

Solomon, A., Haaga, D.A.F., Brody, C., Kirk, L., & Friedman, D.G. (1998). Priming irrational beliefs in recovered-depressed people. *Journal of Abnormal Psychology, 107*, 440–449.

Swann, W.B., Wenzlaff, R.M., Krull, D.S., & Pelham, B.W. (1992). Allure of negative feedback: Self-verification strivings among depressed persons. *Journal of Abnormal Psychology, 101*, 293–306.

Taylor, S.E., & Brown, J.D. (1988). Illusion and well-being: A social psychological perspective on mental health. *Psychological Bulletin, 103*, 193–210.

van den Hout, M., Merckelbach, H., & Pool, K. (1996). Dissociation, reality monitoring, trauma, and thought suppression. *Behavioural and Cognitive Psychotherapy, 24*, 97–108.

Vredenburg, K., Flett, G.L., Krames, L. (1993). Analogue versus clinical depression: A critical reappraisal. *Psychological Bulletin, 113*, 327–344.

Weary, G., Edwards, J.A., & Jacobson, J.A. (1995). Depression research methodologies in the *Journal of Personality and Social Psychology*: A reply. *Journal of Personality and Social Psychology, 68*, 885–891.

Wegner, D.M. (1994). Ironic processes of mental control. *Psychological Review, 101*, 34–52.

Wegner, D.M., & Wenzlaff, R.M. (1996). Mental Control. In E.T. Higgins & A.W. Kruglanski (Eds.), *Social psychology: Handbook of basic principles* (pp. 466–492). New York: Guilford Press.

Wegner, D.M., & Zanakos, S. (1994). Chronic thought suppression. *Journal of Personality, 62*, 615–640.

Weissman, A.N. (1979). The Dysfunctional Attitude Scale: A validation study (Doctoral dissertation, University of Pennsylvania, 1978). *Dissertation Abstracts International, 40*, 1389–1390B.

Weissman, A.N., & Beck A.T. (1978). *Development and validation of the Dysfunctional Attitude Scale: A preliminary investigation*. Paper presented at the annual meeting of the American Educational Research Association, Toronto, Ontario.

Wenzlaff, R.M., & Bates, D.E. (1998). Unmasking a cognitive vulnerability to depression: How lapses in mental control reveal depressive thinking. *Journal of Personality and Social Psychology, 75*, 1559–1571.

Wenzlaff, R.M., & Eisenberg, A.R. (2001). Mental control after dysphoria: Evidence of a suppressed, depressive bias. *Behavior Therapy, 32*, 27–45.

Wenzlaff, R.M., Rude, S.S., Taylor, C.J., Stultz, C.H., Sweatt, R.A. (2001). Beneath the veil of thought suppression: Attentional bias and depression risk. *Cognition and Emotion, 15*, 435–452.

Wenzlaff, R.M., Rude, S.S., & West, L.M. (in press). Cognitive vulnerability to depression: The role of thought suppression and attitude certainty. *Cognition and Emotion*.

Wenzlaff, R.M., & Wegner, D.M. (2000). Thought Suppression. *Annual Review of Psychology, 51,* 59–91.

Wenzlaff, R.M., Wegner, D.M., & Roper, D.W. (1988). Depression and mental control: The resurgence of unwanted negative thoughts. *Journal of Personality and Social Psychology, 55,* 882–892.

Zimmerman, M., & Coryell, W. (1987). The inventory to diagnose depression, lifetime version. *Acta Psychiatrical Scandinavia, 75,* 495–499.

Zuroff, D.C., Colussy, S.A., Wielgus, M.S. (1983). Selective memory and depression: A cautionary note concerning response bias. *Cognitive Therapy and Research, 7,* 223–231.

COGNITION AND EMOTION, 2002, 16 (3), 423–440

Negative processing biases predict subsequent depressive symptoms

Stephanie S. Rude

University of Texas at Austin, USA

Richard M. Wenzlaff

University of Texas at San Antonio, USA

Bryce Gibbs, Jennifer Vane, and Tavia Whitney

University of Texas at Austin, USA

This study investigated the possible relationship between negative processing biases and subsequent depression. The Scrambled Sentences Test (SST), a measure of processing bias, was administered to a large sample of undergraduates. Participants also completed self-report measures of thought suppression tendencies, current level of depression, and lifetime worst-depression symptoms. High scores on the SST, reflecting a negative processing bias, predicted depression symptoms measured 4 to 6 weeks later, even after controlling for concurrent and past depression. The SST was administered both with and without cognitive load to all participants. The SST with load predicted subsequent depression for both men and women. The SST without load predicted depression for women only. The SST difference score, a measure of the change in scores between the no-load and load conditions, was a significant predictor of subsequent depression for men but not women. Among men, the combination of high thought suppression with either high SST-load scores or high SST difference scores proved to be a particularly strong indicator of vulnerability to subsequent depression.

It is well established that depressed individuals tend to focus their attention on unhappy and unflattering information, to interpret information negatively, and to harbour pervasively pessimistic beliefs (e.g., Hollon, Kendall, & Lumry, 1986; Krantz & Rude, 1984; Rude, Krantz, & Rosenhan, 1988). The distinctive claim of cognitive models of depression is that negative thinking is not only a concomitant or symptom of depression—it is also a causal antecedent of

Correspondence should be addressed to Stephanie S. Rude, SZB504, University of Texas, Austin, Texas, 78712, USA; e-mail: Stephanie.rude@mail.utexas.edu; srude@austin.rr.com depression. According to Aaron Beck (1967), for example, depressed and depression-prone individuals possess deep-level assumptive structures (depressive schemas and dysfunctional beliefs) that give rise to consciously accessible depressive thinking ("automatic thoughts"). Depressive schemas, according to Beck, may be dormant or inactive at times but, when activated by difficult life circumstances, such as interpersonal losses, may bring about syndromal depression.

It has been surprisingly difficult to document the existence of "latent" depressive schemas in recovered individuals—the majority of studies that have compared formerly and never-depressed individuals have failed to find group differences in depressive biases (e.g., Gotlib & Cane, 1987; Hollon et al., 1986; Silverman, Silverman, & Eardley, 1984; Wilkinson & Blackburn, 1981; but also see Teasdale & Dent, 1987; Williams & Nulty, 1986). Because formerly depressed individuals are at high risk for relapse (Judd, 1997), they should be especially likely to possess depressive schema, and therefore these results seemed to fly in the face of Beck's cognitive theory of depression.

The lack of evidence for negative biases challenges our cognitive explanations of depression. In fact, these results could be interpreted as indicating that negative thinking is nothing more than a symptom of depression, much like insomnia or difficulty concentrating. These results have also been disappointing because the ability to detect vulnerability out-of-episode would offer a promising tool for etiological research and for early intervention and/or prevention efforts.

It has recently been argued that detection of depressive cognitions in vulnerable individuals requires particular measurement conditions. Various approaches to capturing evidence of depressive processing in vulnerable individuals have been tried, and several of these have proven useful. For example, a fairly large number of recent studies supports the claim that sad mood priming facilitates observation of negative processing among formerly depressed individuals (Ingram, Bernet, & McLaughlin, 1994; Ingram, Miranda, & Segal, 1998; Miranda, Persons, & Byers, 1990). Presumably, the mood priming activates associations to the latent depressive biases, making them more accessible.

The detection of latent depressive biases, however, may not depend on the induction of a sad mood. Rude and Wenzlaff and their colleagues have presented evidence that measurement techniques that reduce respondents' volitional control may enhance observation of negative processing among formerly depressed individuals. For example, Wenzlaff and Bates (1998) found elevated levels of negative solutions on the Scrambled Sentences Test (SST), and Wenzlaff, Rude, Taylor, Stultz, and Sweatt (2001) found more negative word identifications on the Imbedded Word Task (IWT) among formerly depressed versus never-depressed college students when the tasks were performed under cognitive load. In addition to the effects of cognitive load, the nature of processing tasks such as these probably tends to bypass volitional control because the indices of negative processing are incidental to the respondents' task goals (forming coherent sentences, for example) and because the tasks are performed under time pressure. Using clinically diagnosed samples of formerly depressed individuals, Hedlund and Rude (1995) and Rude, Covich, Jarrold, Hedlund, and Zentner (2001) detected negative biases even in the absence of load using the SST and an incidental recall test but did not find biases using questionnaire measures of depressive thinking.

This recent evidence of depressive biases among individuals with a history of depression has provided important support for cognitive models of depression vulnerability. Evidence that processing biases occur not only *during*, but also *following*, depressive episodes has supported the claim that these biases play a role in bringing about depression—that they are not merely effects or concomitants of other depressive symptoms.

However, such evidence is still limited by being cross-sectional. It does not preclude the possibility that cognitive biases observed in remitted individuals are nothing more than inert "scars" of the disorder, persisting effects that have no functional role in vulnerability (cf. Lewinsohn, Steinmetz, Larson, & Franklin, 1981). As Coyne (1992) has argued, priming may merely make accessible "...memories of the profound life experience associated with having spent long periods being depressed..." (also cited in Ingram et al., 1998, p. 234). Clearly, there is a need for prospective data to more strongly support a causal role for biased cognitions in bringing about depression—whether recurrences or first onsets.

To date, a small but growing body of studies supports the claim that negative beliefs and/or cognitive biases predict future occurrences of depressive symptoms (e.g., Alloy Abramson, & Francis, 1999; Lewinsohn, Allen, Seeley, & Gotlib (1999); Metalsky, Abramson, Seligman, Semmel, & Peterson, 1982; Nolen-Hoeksema, Girgus, & Seligman, 1992; Segal, Gemar, & Williams, 1999). In one of the more elegant prospective studies, Segal et al. (1999) followed up individuals who had completed treatment for depression by either cognitive-behaviour therapy or pharmacotherapy. Relapse over a 1–4 year follow-up period was predicted by participants' dysfunctional attitudes reported immediately after a sad mood induction but was not predicted by dysfunctional attitudes reported prior to this mood induction. This study supports the notion that proclivities toward negative thinking are more readily observed in the presence of sad mood and that these otherwise hidden tendencies predict subsequent depression. Although all 54 of the participants in this study were clinically improved, there was still considerable variation in their symptom levels at the time that dysfunctional attitudes were assessed. The failure to control for symptom level in the ·regression equations might be regarded as a limitation of the study. Nevertheless, preliminary support for the role of cognitive bias in predicting subsequent depression is promising.

Despite the insights gained from the prospective studies mentioned above, the findings are limited by the fact that they have relied exclusively on self-report questionnaires to measure cognitive biases. Questionnaire methods are subject to demand and self-presentational effects, and as numerous researchers (e.g., Rector, Segal, & Gemar, 1998; Roberts, Gilboa, & Gotlib, 1998; Segal, 1988) have noted, the use of self-report questionnaires needs to be supplemented with measures that allow observation of biased processing.

In the present study, negative biases were assessed in a large sample of undergraduates using the SST (Wenzlaff, 1988). Depressive symptomatology was assessed at Time 1 and again, 4–6 weeks later. The primary interest was in determining whether negative biases would predict subsequent depression, over and above the prediction offered by concurrent depressive symptoms and reports of worst lifetime depression symptoms. In addition, we were interested in whether a cognitive load manipulation would facilitate the predictive effects of the negative bias task among participants who reported a tendency to suppress negative thinking. A large body of research indicates that cognitive demands can disrupt thought suppression, allowing unwanted thoughts to exert greater influence (for a review, see Wenzlaff & Wegner, 2000). If formerly depressed individuals are trying to suppress their depressive biases, then a load should disrupt their efforts and reveal the underlying cognitions (Beevers, Wenzlaff, Hayes, & Scott, 1999; Wenzlaff, 1993).

METHOD

Participants and procedure

Packets that included the measures described below were administered to undergraduates at the University of Texas at Austin, who participated as a means of fulfilling requirements of their introductory psychology class. A total of 339 students (253 women and 86 men) with a mean age of 18.34 years (SD = 2.09 years) completed the packets in groups during two data collection phases spaced 4 to 6 weeks apart. In the first session participants completed the Beck Depression Inventory (BDI), the Inventory to Diagnose Depression-Lifetime, the White Bear Suppression Inventory, and the SST. In the second session participants completed the BDI again. Although the packets included measures other than those reported here, the measures used in the present study appeared in the packets in the ordering given below.[1]

Measures

The Beck Depression Inventory   (BDI; Beck, Ward, Mendelson, Mock, & Erbaugh, 1961) was used to measure participants' level of depression at Time 1 and Time 2. The BDI is a widely used self-report inventory of depressive symptoms with good internal consistency and test-retest reliability. BDI scores have been shown to correlate highly with psychiatrist ratings of depression (Bumberry, Oliver, & McClure, 1978) and with the interviewer-administered Hamilton Rating Scale for Depression in a college sample (Hammen, 1980).

The Inventory to Diagnose Depression   (IDD-L; Zimmerman & Coryell, 1987) was used to assess the severity of the worst prior episode of depression. Respondents are asked to recall the most depressed week in their lives and on each of 22 items, to select a statement best describing how they felt, and to indicate whether they felt that way for more or less than two weeks. Only symptoms reported for greater than two weeks duration are included in the total score. The IDD-L has been shown to have good discriminant validity (Sakado, Sato, Uehara, Sato, & Kameda, 1996) and test-retest reliability (Sato et al., 1996). It is also comparable to the Diagnostic Interview Schedule (Zimmerman & Coryell, 1987) with regard to sensitivity and specificity.

The White Bear Suppression Inventory   (WBSI; Wegner & Zanakos, 1994) was used to assess participants' tendency to suppress unwanted negative thoughts. The WBSI is a 15-item self-report inventory with items such as "Sometimes I wonder why I have the thoughts I do" and "I always try to put

---

[1] Participants received one of two questionnaire packets that differed in the order in which measures were administered. Half of the four group administration sessions received each order. 159 (122 women and 37 men) participants received the following ordering of questionnaires: BDI; Pilot version of Imbedded Words Test (IWF, Wenzlaff et al., 2001); Scrambled Sentences Test (SST); Dysfunctional Attitudes Scale (DAS; Weissman, 1979); Automatic Thoughts Questionnaire (ATQ; Hollon & Kendall, 1980); Pilot version of Adjective Self-Description Task (ASDT); Trait Meta-Mood Scale (TMMS; Salovey, Mayer, Goldman, Turvey, & Palfai, 1995); Inventory to Diagnose Depression-Lifetime (IDD-L); White Bear Suppression Inventory (WBSI). 180 (131 women and 49 men) participants received the following ordering of questionnaires: BDI; DAS; ATQ; Pilot IWF; SST; ASDT; TMMS; IDD-L; WBSI. Of participants receiving the first questionnaire sequence, 85 (67 women and 18 men) received the first block of the SST under load and the remaining 88 (67 women and 21 men) received the second block of the SST under load. Of participants receiving the second questionnaire sequence, 85 (63 women and 22 men) received the first block of the SST under load and the remaining 81 (56 women and 25 men) received the second block of the SST under load. Ordering of the measures was not associated with differences on any of the variables and did not interact with study variables in predicting subsequent depression symptoms.

problems out of mind.'' Respondents rate each item using a 5-point Likert scale (1, strongly disagree; 5, strongly agree). Total scores range from 15 to 75, with higher scores representing higher levels of thought suppression. The WBSI has also been shown to have strong internal consistency and test-retest reliability (Muris, Merckelbach, & Horselenberg, 1996). Factor analysis of the WBSI yielded a one-factor solution. The WBSI appears to be highly correlated with self-report measures of trait-anxiety, neuroticism, depression, obsessive-compulsive symptomology, and intrusive thinking (Muris et al., 1996).

The Scrambled Sentences Test (SST; Wenzlaff, 1988, 1993) was used to measure participants' tendency to interpret ambiguous information (e.g., ''winner born I am loser a'') in positive (''I am a born winner'') or negative (''I am a born loser'') ways. Several studies (Hedlund & Rude, 1995; Rude et al., 2001; Wenzlaff, 1988; Wenzlaff & Bates, 1998) have shown differences between formerly depressed and never-depressed groups on this task. As Wenzlaff has done in prior studies, participants were presented with a list of scrambled sentences and instructed to write a number above five of the six words of each scrambled sentence to produce a grammatically correct sentence. Participants were presented with two blocks of 20 sentences and given 2.5 min to complete each block. They were instructed to complete as many of the sentences as possible during this period. A ''negativity'' score for each block was produced by calculating the ratio of negative sentences over total sentences completed (of 20 possible).

As in prior uses of the SST (e.g., Wenzlaff, 1993), a cognitive load procedure was used in either the first or the second block of sentences administered to each participant. In the cognitive load condition participants were given a six-digit number to remember while they were doing the task. Although size of the load was not calibrated for each individual, the current procedure has the advantage of allowing group administration and has been shown in prior studies to produce predicted effects (Wenzlaff & Wegner, 2000).

In the present study, participants completed one block of 20 sentences under cognitive load (SST-load) and one without load (SST-no load). Order of the load and no load conditions was varied across the group administration sessions, with roughly half of participants ($n = 171$; 130 women and 41 men) completing the first block of scrambled sentences under load. For the block of sentences completed under load, participants were asked to write the six-digit load number at the bottom of their answer sheet at the end of the 2.5 min period; 88% of participants reported the number with perfect accuracy.[2]

---

[2] Eliminating data from those participants who made errors in their recall of the digits did not change the pattern of results.

RESULTS

Description of the sample

Means and standard deviations for each of the variables included in analyses are given in Table 1. Because depression scores are frequently observed to vary as a function of gender, means are shown for men and women separately, as well as for the combined sample; t-test comparisons between the men and women are also shown. Table 2 shows correlations among these variables for men and women and for the total sample. As can be seen from Tables 1 and 2, respectively, several of the means and several of the correlations (shown in boldface) were significantly different between men and women in the sample.

Effects of cognitive load, suppression tendency, and gender on SST negative bias

The purpose of the cognitive load manipulation was to disable participants' tendency to suppress negative solutions on the SST. Hence, we anticipated that, for high-suppressing participants, the SST score would be higher (more negative) under load than without load. We were also interested in determining whether gender would be associated with differences in SST scores. To address these questions we used mixed model analysis of variance to compare SST score under load versus no-load (a within-subjects factor). Suppression tendency

TABLE 1
Means (and standard deviations) on study variables for men, women, and for the sample as a whole

	Women (n = 253)		Men (n = 86)		Combined (n = 339)		Comparison of genders (t)
	Mean	(SD)	Mean	(SD)	Mean	(SD)	
BDI-T1	6.34	(5.87)	5.06	(5.00)	6.01	(5.68)	−1.96**
BDI-T2	6.63	(6.62)	5.36	(5.99)	6.31	(6.48)	−1.66*
IDD-L	15.84	(16.80)	11.94	(12.75)	14.85	(15.95)	−2.25**
WBSI	50.19	(10.18)	49.67	(10.03)	50.06	(10.13)	−0.41
SST-Load	0.09	(0.14)	0.15	(0.20)	0.11	(0.16)	2.38**
SST-No-load	0.11	(0.16)	0.12	(0.15)	0.11	(0.15)	0.80
SST-Diff	−0.02	(0.12)	0.02	(0.13)	−0.01	(0.13)	2.39**

BDI-T1, Beck Depression Inventory (BDI) score at Time 1; BDI-T2, BDI score at Time 2; IDD-L, Inventory to Diagnose Depression–Lifetime; WBSI, White Bear Suppression Inventory; SST-Load, Scrambled Sentences Test (SST) performed under cognitive load; SST-No-load, SST performed without load; SST-Diff, The difference score calculated as SST-Load minus SST-No-load. The SST is scored by calculating the ratio of negative solution sentences over the number of sentences solved in each 20-item block. *, $p < .10$; **, $p < .05$ (2-tailed).

TABLE 2

Correlations among major variables for the total sample and for men and women separately

	BDI-T2	IDD-L	WBSI	SST-Load	SST-No-load	SST-Diff
BDI-T1	.60	.39	.48	.51[c]	.55[b]	.02
Women	(.60)	(.40)	(.46)	(.59)	(.61)	(−.08)
Men	(.58)	(.32)	(.54)	(.41)	(.41)	(−.24)
BDI-T2		.34	.41	.48[c]	.46	.04[a]
Women		(.34)	(.39)	(.45)	(.48)	(−.09)
Men		(.31)	(.48)	(.62)	(.39)	(−.47)
IDD-L			.32	.25	.27	.01
Women			(.35)	(.29)	(.29)	(−.02)
Men			(.22)	(.26)	(.23)	(.17)
WBSI				.33	.28	.10[b]
Women				(.29)	(.25)	(.04)
Men				(.45)	(.38)	(.28)
SST-Load					.67	.44[a]
Women					(.67)	(.32)
Men					(.71)	(.64)
SST-No-load						−.38[a]
Women						(−.50)
Men						(−.06)

Note: Significance of the difference between each pair of correlations for men and for women was calculated using Fisher's *r* to *z* transformation. For those instances in which the correlations for men and women were significantly different, the overall correlation coefficient (for the total sample) is shown in boldface with a notation: A superscript a, b, or c indicates that the correlations for men and women were significant different at (2-tailed) alpha = .01, .05, or .10, respectively. The critical values of *r* for testing the difference of the correlations from zero using a 2-tailed alpha of .01, .05, and .10, respectively, are r_{crit} = .25, .20, and .16 for both the total sample (*n* = 339) and for women (*n* = 253), and r_{crit} = .28, .20, and .18 for men (*n* = 86).

(above or below the median on the WBSI) and gender were between-subjects factors. Means and standard deviations for SST scores as a function of gender and suppression group are shown in Table 3.

Because only high suppressors (above the median on the WBSI) were expected to perform differently on the SST as a function of load condition, no main effect was expected for the cognitive load manipulation, and none was found, $F(1, 335) < 1.0$. There was a main effect for suppression group (above or below the median on the WBSI), $F(1, 335) = 30.52$, $p < .001$. High-suppressing participants produced more negative solutions on the SST, overall. As Wenzlaff (1993) has reported previously, WBSI score correlates fairly highly with depressed mood and therefore with higher scores on the SST. Despite the fact that high scorers on the WBSI report trying to suppress negative thoughts and feelings, they appear not to completely suppress negative solutions on the SST, even in the absence of cognitive load.

TABLE 3
Mean proportion negative sentences under load and no load
for men and women above and below the median on thought
suppression (WBSI)

	n	Cognitive load	No load
Women			
High suppressors	133	.13 (0.17)	.14 (0.18)
Low suppressors	120	.05 (0.10)	.07 (0.11)
Men			
High suppressors	39	.22 (0.23)	.17 (0.16)
Low suppressors	47	.08 (0.13)	.08 (0.13)

Note: The median WBSI score (51) for the sample was used to create high and low suppression groups. Standard deviations are given in parentheses.

There was also a main effect for gender, $F(1, 335) = 6.05$, $p < .01$: Men produced higher SST scores than did women. Further, gender interacted with cognitive load condition, $F(1, 335) = 7.03$, $p < .01$. Men's tendency toward greater negativity was most pronounced in the cognitive load condition. The predicted two-way interaction between cognitive load condition and suppression group fell just short of being statistically significant, $F(1, 335) = 3.43$, $p = .07$, as did the three-way interaction of cognitive load condition, suppression group, and gender, $F(1, 335) = 3.20$, $p = .08$. Examination of the means in Table 3 reveals that only men showed the predicted pattern whereby high suppressors produced more negative SST solutions under cognitive load than without load. In an auxiliary analysis that included only men, the interaction between suppression group and cognitive load condition was significant, $F(1, 84) = 4.11$, $p < .05$. Men in this sample responded to the cognitive load procedure as expected (and as previously found by Wenzlaff, 1993) but women did not.

Overview of analyses for predicting depression

The relationship between the degree of negative bias that participants showed on the SST and their subsequent depression symptoms was examined using hierarchical multiple regression equations with BDI score at Time 2 as the criterion variable. In each regression, BDI score at Time 1 and IDD-L score were entered in the first step in order to control for concurrent and lifetime symptom reports, respectively. The cognitive load and no-load versions of the test were examined in separate regressions, identical except with respect to the version of the SST entered. Separate regressions were used to evaluate SST-load and SST-no-load because the interest was in knowing whether *each* version (by itself) predicted subsequent depression. Comparison of the load and no-load versions was accomplished in a subsequent regression using the difference between SST score under each condition. In each regression, the utility of the SST predictor was evaluated by testing the significance of the increase in the R^2 resulting from its addition to the model containing BDI at Time 1 and IDD-L scores.

Because men and women differed, not only in mean scores on several variables, but also in the relationships between key variables, we analysed the prediction data for men and women separately.[3]

Does negative bias on the Scrambled Sentences Test (SST) predict subsequent depression symptoms?

Male participants.   Using male participants only, BDI score at Time 1 (β = .54, $p < .001$), and IDD-L score (β = .11, $p = .25$), were entered into an equation predicting BDI score at Time 2. The combination of these two variables, which reflect current and past depression symptoms, respectively, accounted for 35% of the variance in BDI scores at Time 2. The addition of SST-load to this equation accounted for an additional 14% of the variance, a statistically significant increase in R^2, $F(1, 82) = 21.75$, $p < .001$. In the parallel equation in which SST-no-load score was added to the model containing BDI from Time 1 and IDD-L, only an additional 2% of the variance in BDI scores at Time 2 was accounted for ($p = .12$).

Female participants.   Using female participants only, BDI score at Time 1 (β = .55, $p < .001$), and IDD-L score (β = .12, $p < .05$), were entered into an equation predicting BDI score at Time 2. The combination of these two variables, which reflect current and past depression symptoms, respectively, accounted for 38% of the variance in BDI scores at Time 2. The addition of SST-load accounted for an additional 1% of the variance, a small but statistically significant increase, $F(1, 249) = 4.34$, $p < .05$. In the parallel equation in which SST-no-load score was added to the model containing BDI from Time 1 and

---

[3] Gender did not moderate the effects of SST-load or SST-no-load in predicting depression. However, the effect of the SST difference score was moderated by gender (the interaction accounted for an additional 2% of the variance for the model that already included Time 1 BDI and IDD-L score, gender, and the SST difference score, $F(1, 337) = 3.40$, $p < .01$). Since gender was not a significant moderator of the effects of SST-load and SST-no load, the reader may be interested to know that when the total sample (men and women included) was used to evaluate the effects of SST-load and SST-no-load in predicting Time 2 depression (as was done for men and women separately), both were statistically significant. Using the whole sample, SST-load contributed an additional 3% to the R^2, for the model that already included Time 1 BDI and IDD-L score, $F(1, 337) = 16.46, p < .001$, and SST-no-load added an additional 2% to the R^2 for this model, $F(1, 337) = 9.46$, $p < .01$.

IDD-L, an additional 2% of the variance in BDI scores at Time 2 was accounted for, $F(1, 249) = 7.41, p < .05$.

Does the addition of cognitive load enhance prediction of depression?

In order to assess the differential utility of the two administration conditions for the SST, a new variable, SST difference score, was created: SST-no-load score was subtracted from SST-load score for each participant. The resulting difference score reflected the degree to which SST score under cognitive load was more negative than SST without load. The importance of this index is that it reflects the degree to which negativity is "unmasked" by the load condition.

Male participants.   Analytic procedures were parallel to those described above: SST difference score was added to the equation that already contained scores for BDI at Time 1 and IDD-L. The inclusion of the SST difference score accounted for an additional 11% of the variance in Time 2 BDI scores, $F(1, 82) = 16.90, p < .001$. This is consistent with the findings that SST-load score but not SST-no load score predicted subsequent depression for men.

Female participants.   The addition of the SST difference score did not add to the variance accounted for in Time 2 BDI scores, $p > .4$. Again, this is consistent with the fact that, for women, SST scores under *both* load and no-load conditions predicted subsequent depression to a small degree.

Does suppression tendency moderate the predictive effects of the SST?

In the following analyses' self-reported suppression tendency (WBSI score) and its associated interactions were added as predictors to each of the three-predictor models examined above. Our interest was in determining whether suppression tendency, itself, adds to the prediction of subsequent depression, as well as whether suppression tendency interacts with negative processing biases (SST scores) in predicting depression. WBSI score was added as a fourth predictor to each of the models evaluated above and the significance of the R^2 change in predicting Time 2 BDI at this step was assessed. Finally, the contribution of the two-way interaction between WBSI score and the relevant SST score to the model was evaluated.

Male participants.   Adding WBSI score to the model that included scores for BDI at Time 1, IDD-L, and SST-load, accounted for a nonsignificant 1% additional variance in the prediction of Time 2 BDI, $p > .2$. The interaction between WBSI and SST-load did account for an additional 7% of the variance, $F(1, 80) = 13.67, p < .001$.

When WBSI score was added to the three-predictor model that included SST scores from the no-load condition, it accounted for an additional 3% of the variance, $F(1, 81) = 4.34$, $p < .05$. Adding the interaction between WBSI score and SST-no-load score in a subsequent step accounted for slightly less than 1% additional variance, $p > .3$.

Adding WBSI score to the model that included the SST difference score accounted for an additional 2% of the variance, $p = .08$. The interaction between WBSI score and SST-difference score accounted for an additional 19% of the variance in Time 2 BDI scores, $F(1, 80) = 45.39$, $p < .001$. This interaction indicates that (for men) the combined influence of tendency to suppress negative thinking and a high rate of negativity on the load, as compared to the no-load version of the SST, was associated with subsequent depression.

Female participants.   Adding WBSI score to the model that included scores for BDI at Time 1, IDD-L, and SST-load, accounted for a small but statistically significant 1% additional variance in the prediction of Time 2 BDI, $F(1, 248) = 4.22$, $p < .05$. The interaction between WBSI and SST-load, added in the next step, did not account for any additional variance, $p > .5$.

When WBSI score was added to the three-predictor model that included SST score from the no-load condition, it accounted for an additional 1% of the variance, $F(1, 248) = 5.29$, $p < .05$. Addition of the interaction between WBSI score and SST-no-load in the next step did not account for any additional variance, $p > .5$.

Finally, adding WBSI score to the model that included SST-difference score accounted for a small but statistically significant 1% of the variance, $F(1, 248) = 4.74$, $p < .05$. Adding the interaction between WBSI score and SST-difference score did not account for any additional variance in Time 2 BDI scores, $p > .5$.

DISCUSSION

These results support the theoretical claim made by cognitive models of depression that negative processing biases—in this case, biases in resolving ambiguous verbal information—predict subsequent symptoms of depression. Importantly, this result was obtained while controlling for concurrent symptoms of depression (Time 1 BDI scores) *and* reported worst lifetime symptoms of depression (IDD-L scores). This is important since the number and severity of prior depressions has been the single best predictor of subsequent depression in research to date. Although the IDD-L does not establish the number of prior episodes of depression, it does provide an index of the severity of past depressive experiences. The importance of negative processing biases in predicting subsequent depression is clearly indicated by the predictive power of the SST as shown in this study. The contribution of SST scores was significant even after controlling for past and concurrent depressive symptoms. Although we cannot definitively conclude that negative biases cause subsequent depressive symptoms, the pattern of these results makes the claim for causality compelling. If these biases were nothing more than inert "scars" of past experiences of dysphoria or depression, they would not be expected to add uniquely to the prediction of subsequent depression symptoms.

A clear understanding of these data requires separate consideration of male and female participants. First, men's SST scores, overall, were significantly higher than those of women. Yet, despite their higher SST scores, men's scores on the self-report measures of distress (both BDI administrations and the IDD-L) were lower than those of women; and men's scores on the WBSI were no different than those of women. It is possible that the discrepancy between the pattern shown by the self-report measures (the BDI, IDD-L, and WBSI scores) and the processing measures (the SST scores) reflects different self-presentation strategies used by men and women. In other words, men may have a higher threshold than women for describing their experiences in negative terms on self-report measures; yet their experiences or perceptions, as reflected by processing measures (SST scores in the present instance) may be as negative or more negative than those of women. Under this view, the very same mental control attempts that led men to report *more* negative interpretations when handicapped by the cognitive load manipulation may have led them to under-report depressive symptoms and suppression tendencies (because volitional control was not disabled on the latter inventories). Note that this explanation does not require a hypothesis of intentional deception—self-report inventories require respondents to quantify their experience and hence are subject to anchoring and estimation biases.

Another possible reason for the discrepancy between SST negativity and BDI is that men's initial processing is more negative than that of women but their subsequent behaviour or processing makes them less vulnerable to experiencing depression as a result. For example, women's tendency to ruminate more about distressing experiences, as documented by Nolen-Hoeksema (1987), may be the intervening variable that puts them at greater risk for depression, despite lower levels of perceiving negative information compared to men.

Importantly, men also differed from women in their response to the cognitive load manipulation. Cognitive load clearly seemed to "unmask" a negative bias among the men—SST-load scores of high-suppressing men were clearly higher than their SST-no-load scores. This is consistent with the interpretation that cognitive load helps disable volitional attempts to suppress negative interpretations.

These differences in the degree of negative bias on the load and no-load versions of the SST shown by men were mirrored in the prediction of subsequent depression: SST-load score predicted subsequent depression but SST-no-load score did not. It appears that, for men, better prediction of depression is obtained by a cognitive load procedure that interferes with volitional responding. Both the

university population using psychiatric estimate as the criterion. *Journal of Consulting and Clinical Psychology, 46,* 150–155.

Coyne, J.C. (1992). Cognition in depression: A paradigm in crisis. *Psychological Inquiry, 3,* 232–235.

Gotlib, I.H., & Cane, D.B. (1987). Construct accessibility and clinical depression: A longitudinal investigation. *Journal of Abnormal Psychology, 96,* 199–204.

Hammen, C. (1980). Depression in college students: Beyond the Beck Depression Inventory. *Journal of Consulting and Clinical Psychology, 48,* 126–128.

Hedlund, S., & Rude, S.S. (1995). Evidence of latent depressive schemata in formerly depressed individuals. *Journal of Abnormal Psychology, 104,* 517–525.

Hollon, S.D., & Kendall, P.C. (1980). Cognitive self-statements in depression: Development of an automatic thoughts questionnaire. *Cognitive Therapy and Research, 4,* 383–395.

Hollon, S.D., Kendall, P.C., & Lumry, A. (1986). Specificity of depressotypic cognitions in clinical depression. *Journal of Abnormal Psychology, 95,* 52–59.

Ingram, R.E., Bernet, C.Z., & McLaughlin, S.C. (1994). Attention allocation processes in depressed individuals. *Cognitive Therapy and Research, 18,* 317–332.

Ingram, R.E., Miranda, J., & Segal, Z.V. (1998). *Cognitive vulnerability to depression.* New York: Guilford Press.

Islam, S.S., & Schottenfeld, D. (1994). Declining FEV_1 and chronic productive cough in cigarette smokers: A 25-year prospective study of lung cancer incidence in Tecumseh, Michigan. *Cancer Epidemiology, Biomarkers, and Prevention, 3,* 289–298.

Judd, L.L. (1997). The clinical course of unipolar major depressive disorders. *Archives of General Psychiatry, 54,* 989–991.

Krantz, S.E., & Rude, S.S. (1984). Depressive attributions: Selection of different causes or assignment of dimensional meanings? *Journal of Personality and Social Psychology, 47,* 193–203.

Lewinsohn, P.M., Allen, N.B., Seeley, J.R., & Gotlib, I.H. (1999). First onset versus recurrence of depression: Differential processes of psychosocial risk. *Journal of Abnormal Psychology, 108,* 483–489.

Lewinsohn, P.M., Solomon, A., Seeley, J.R., & Zeiss, A. (2000). Clinical implications of "sub-threshold" depressive symptoms. *Journal of Abnormal Psychology, 109,* 345–351.

Lewinsohn, P.M., Steinmetz, L., Larson, D.W., & Franklin, J. (1981). Depression-related cognitions: Antecedents or consequence? *Journal of Abnormal Psychology, 90,* 213–219.

Metalsky, G., Abramson, L.Y., Seligman, M., Semmel, A., & Peterson, C.. (1982). Attributional styles and life events in the classroom: Vulnerabilty and invulnerability to depressive mood reactions. *Journal of Personality and Social Psychology, 43,* 612–617.

Meyer, G.J., Finn, S.E., Eyde, L.D., Kay, G.G., Moreland, K.L., Dies, R.R., Eisman, E.J., Kubiszyn, T.W., & Reed, G.M. (2001). Psychological testing and psychological assessment: A review of evidence and issues. *American Psychologist, 56,* 128–165.

Miranda, J., & Persons, J.B., & Byers, C.N. (1990). Endorsement of dysfunctional beliefs depends on current mood state. *Journal of Abnormal Psychology, 99,* 237–241.

Muris, P., Merckelbach, H., & Horselenberg, R.(1996). Individual differences in thought suppression, the White Bear Suppression Inventory: Factor structure, reliability, validity, and correlates. *Behavior Research and Therapy, 34,* 501–513.

Nolen-Hoeksema, S. (1987). Sex differences in unipolar depression: Evidence and theory. *Psychological Bulletin, 101,* 259–282.

Nolen-Hoeksema, S., Girgus, J.S., & Seligman, M.E.P. (1992). Predictors and consequences of childhood depressive symptoms: A 5-year longitudinal study. *Journal of Abnormal Psychology, 101,* 405–422.

Persons, J.B., & Rao, P.A. (1985). Longitudinal study of cognitions, life events, and depression in psychiatric inpatients. *Journal of Abnormal Psychology, 94,* 51–63.

Rector, N.A., Segal, Z.V., & Gemar, M. (1998). Schema research in depression: A Canadian perspective. *Canadian Journal of Behavioural Science, 30,* 213–224.

Roberts, J.E., Gilboa, E., & Gotlib, I.H. (1998). Ruminative response style and vulnerability to episodes dysphoria: Gender, neuroticism, and episode duration. *Cognitive Therapy and Research, 22,* 401–423.

Rude, S.S., Covich, J., Jarrold, W., Hedlund, S., & Zentner, M. (2001). Detecting depressive schemata in vulnerable individuals: Questionnaires versus laboratory tasks. *Cognitive Therapy and Research, 25,* 103–116.

Rude, S.S., Krantz, S.E., & Rosenhan, D.L. (1988). Distinguishing the dimensions of valence and belief consistency in depressive and nondepressive information processing. *Cognitive Therapy and Research, 12,* 391–407.

Sakado, K., Sato, T., Uehara, T., Sato, S., Kameda, K. (1996). Discriminant validity of the Inventory to Diagnose Depression, Lifetime Version. *Acta Psychiatra Scandinavia, 93,* 257–260.

Salovey, P., Mayer, J.D., Goldman, S.L., Turvey, C., & Palfai, T.P. (1995). Emotional attention, clarity, and repair: Exploring emotional intelligence using the trait meta-mood scale. In J. W. Pennebaker (Ed.), *Emotion, disclosure, and health,* (pp. 125–154). Washington, DC: American Psychological Association.

Sato, T., Uehara, T., Sakado, K., Sato, S., Nishioka, K., & Kasahara, Y. (1996). The test-retest reliability of the Inventory to Diagnose Depression, Lifetime Version. *Psychopathology, 29,* 154–158.

Segal, Z.V. (1988). Appraisal of the self-schema construct in cognitive models of depression. *Psychological Bulletin, 103,* 147–162.

Segal, Z.V., Gemar, M., & Williams, S. (1999). Differential cognitive response to a mood challenge following successful cognitive therapy or pharmacotherapy for unipolar depression. *Journal of Abnormal Psychology, 108,* 3–10.

Silverman, J.S., Silverman, J.A., & Eardley, D.A. (1984). Do maladaptive attitudes cause depression? *Archives of General Psychiatry, 41,* 28–30.

Teasdale, J.D., & Dent, J. (1987). Cognitive vulnerability to depression: An investigation of two hypotheses. *British Journal of Clinical Psychology, 26,* 113–126.

Wegner, D.M., & Zanakos, S. (1994). Chronic thought suppression. *Journal of Personality, 62,* 615–640.

Weissman, A.N. (1979). *The Dysfunctional Attitude Scale: A validation study* (Doctoral dissertation, University of Pennsylvania, 1978). *Dissertation Abstracts International, 40,* 1389–1390B.

Wenzlaff, R.M. (1988, May) *Automatic information processing in depression.* Paper presented at the International Conference on Self-Control, Nags Head, NC.

Wenzlaff, R.M. (1993). The mental control of depression: Psychological obstacles to emotional well-being. In D.M. Wegner & J.W. Pennebaker(Eds.), *Handbook of mental control* (pp. 239–257). Englewood Cliffs, NJ: Prentice Hall.

Wenzlaff, R.M., & Bates, D.E. (1998). Unmasking a cognitive vulnerability to depression: How lapses in mental control reveal depressive thinking. *Journal of Personality and Social Psychology, 75,* 1559–1571.

Wenzlaff, R.M., Rude, S.S., Taylor, C.J., Stultz, C.H., & Sweatt, R.A. (2001). Beneath the veil of thought suppression: Attentional bias and depression risk. *Cognition and Emotion, 15,* 435–452.

Wenzlaff, R.M., & Wegner, D.M. (2000). Thought suppression. *Annual Review of Psychology, 51,* 59–91.

Wilkinson, I.M., & Blackburn, I.M. (1981). Cognitive style in depressed and recovered depressed patients. *British Journal of Clinical Psychology, 20,* 283–292.

Williams, J.M.G., & Nulty, D.D. (1986). Construct accessibility, depression and the emotional stroop task: Transient mood or stable structure? *Personality and Individual Differences, 7,* 485–491.

Yusef, S., Zucker, D., Peduzzi, P., Fisher, L.D., Takaro, T. Kennedy, J.W., Davis, K., Killip, T., Passamani, E., Norris, R., Morris, C. Mathur, V., Varnauskas, E., & Chalmers, T.C. (1994). Effect of coronary artery bypass graft surgery on survival: Overview of 10-year results from the randomized trials by the Coronary Artery Bypass Graft Surgery Trialists Collaboration. *Lancet, 344,* 563–570.

Zimmerman, M. & Coryell, (1987). The Inventory to Diagnose Depression, Lifetime Version. *Acta Psychiatrical Scandinavia, 75,* 495–499.

Call for Papers

**A Special Issue of *Cognition and Emotion* will be published
in 2004 on
Emotional Memory Failures
Edited by Ineke Wessel and Daniel Wright**

Cognition and Emotion invites contributions to this Special Issue. Its purpose is to bring together papers examining emotion and memory malleability. The debate on recovered memories of trauma in the beginning of the 90s inspired various lines of inquiry into the mechanisms for how false memories might be created (e.g., memory implanting, false word memory) and also how true memories might be forgotten (e.g., retrieval-induced forgetting). These paradigms however, mainly relied on emotionally neutral material. The forthcoming Special Issue will especially be concerned with the questions of to what extent emotive material can be falsely recalled and forgotten and whether there are special populations more susceptible to these effects. Articles can present empirical studies, literature reviews, or theoretical models.

All submissions will be refereed, and any submitted manuscripts with content deemed by the Guest Editors to be outside of the scope of the Special Issue will be reviewed as regular submissions to the journal.

Potential contributors are invited to explore topics by sending emails to either Ineke Wessel at I.Wessel@PSYCHOLOGY.UNIMAAS.NL or Daniel Wright at DanW@Cogs.Susx.ac.uk

Manuscripts for the Special Issue should be submitted no later than 1 December 2002, and they should include a cover letter indicating clearly that they are intended to be considered for the Special Issue.

Submission of manuscripts through electronic mail (preferably as RTF attachments) to Ineke Wessel is especially encouraged. Alternatively, please submit five copies and an electronic version (RTF format on PC-compatible floppydisk) of the manuscript (following APA guidelines) to Ineke Wessel, Experimental Psychology, Department of Psychology, Maastricht University, P.O. Box 616, 6200 MD Maastricht, The Netherlands.

Notes to Authors

MANUSCRIPT SUBMISSION

Manuscripts may be submitted either as hard copies or electronically. Electronic versions of the manuscript should be submitted in Rich Text Format (RTF). They can be emailed as formatted attachments to craig.a.smith@vanderbilt.edu, or they can be mailed on 3.5 inch diskettes accompanied by a single hard copy. Guidelines for the preparation of text and artwork for electronic submission are available from Kirsten Buchanan at: kirsten.buchanan@psypress.co.uk. If just hard copies are submitted, <u>FIVE</u> copies should be sent. Mailed submissions should be sent to Dr. C. Smith, Editor of *Cognition and Emotion*, at the Department of Psychology & Human Development, Vanderbilt University, Box 512, Peabody College, Nashville TN 37203, USA. Please note, all manuscripts submitted should be typed throughout in *double* space, on one side only and with wide margins.

Submission of a paper is taken as acceptance by the author that it contains nothing libellous or infringing copyright. When a paper is accepted for publication, the copyright will belong to the publisher.

FORMAT

Papers should be prepared in the format prescribed by the *American Psychological Association*. For full details of this format, please see the Publication Manual of the *APA* (5th Edition).

Title This should be as concise as possible, and typed on a separate sheet, together with the name(s) of the author(s) and the full postal address(es) of their institution(s). Proofs and requests for reprints will be sent to the first author unless otherwise indicated. A short running title of not more than 40 characters (including spaces) should also be indicated if the title is longer than this.

Abstract An abstract of 100–150 words should follow the title page on a separate sheet.

Headings Indicate headings and sub-headings for different sections of the paper clearly. Do not number headings.

Acknowledgements These should be as brief as possible and typed on a separate sheet at the beginning of the text.

Permission to quote Any direct quotation, regardless of length, must be accompanied by a reference citation that includes a page number. Any quote over six manuscript lines should have formal written permission to quote from the copyright owner. It is the author's responsibility to determine whether permission is required from the copyright owner, and if so, to obtain it.

Footnotes These should be avoided unless absolutely necessary. Essential footnotes should be indicated by superscript figures in the text and collected on a separate sheet at the end of the manuscript.

Reference citations within the text Use authors' last names, with the year of publication in parentheses after the last author's name, for example: Jones and Smith (1987); alternatively: (Brown, 1982; Jones & Smith, 1987; White, Johnson, & Thomas, 1990). On first citation of references with three, four, or five authors, give all names in full, thereafter use first author "et al." Six or more authors are always first author "et al". If more than one article by the same author(s) in the same year is cited, the letters a, b, c etc. should follow the year.

Reference list A full list of references quoted in the text should be given at the end of the paper in alphabetical order of authors' surnames (chronologically for a group of references by the same authors), commencing as a new sheet, typed double spaced. Titles of journals and books should be given in full, as in the following examples:

Books:
Cronbach, L.J., & Gleser, G.C. (1965). Psychological tests and personnel decisions (2nd ed.). Urbana, IL: Glencoe Press.

Chapter in edited book:
Jones, R.R., Reid, J.B., & Patterson, G.R. (1975). Naturalistic observation in clinical assessment. In P. McReynolds (Ed.), Advances in psychological assessment (Vol.3, pp. 234–297). San Francisco, CA: Jossey-Bass.

Journal article:
McReynolds, P. (1979). Interactional assessment. Behavioural Assessment, 1, 237–247.

Tables These should be kept to the minimum. Each table should be typed double spaced on a separate sheet, giving the heading, for example, Table 2, in Arabic numerals, followed by the legend, followed by the table. Make sure that appropriate units are given. Instructions for placing the table should be given in parentheses in the text, for example (Table 2 about here).

Figures Figures should only be used when essential. Where possible, related diagrams should be grouped together to form a single figure. Figures should be drawn to professional standards, and it is recommended that the linear dimensions of figures be approximately twice those intended for the final printed version. (Maximum printed figure size 181 mm x 114 mm, including caption.) Make sure that axes of graphs are properly labelled, and that appropriate units are given. The figure captions should be typed in a separate section, headed, for example, Figure 2, in Arabic numerals. Instructions for placing the figure should be given in parentheses in the text, for example (Figure 2 about here).

Statistics Results of statistical tests should be given in the following form:

$$F(1, 9) = 25.35, p < .001$$

similarly for *t*, and other tests.

Abbreviations Abbreviations should be avoided except in the most standard of cases. Experimental conditions should be named in full, except in tables and figures.

AFTER SUBMISSION
Offprints Contributors receive 50 copies of their printed article free. Additional offprints may be ordered on a form provided by the publishers at the time the proofs are sent to the authors.

New!

CULTURE AND EMOTION

Agneta H. Fischer, Antony S.R. Manstead
(both, University of Amsterdam, The Netherlands) Eds.

For the past three decades theorizing and research on the relationship between culture and emotion has tended to concentrate on the seemingly straightforward issue of whether or not emotions are universal. This was reflected in a dispute in which it seemed only possible to choose between the two extremes, namely a cultural-relativist point of view or a universalist point of view. However, recent empirical evidence concerning cultural variation in emotion has expanded and is generally consistent with the view that an extreme position in this controversy is untenable. Currently, there is abundant research trying to gain insight into the subtleties of cultural effects, rather than in the 'yes' or 'no' issue.

The papers selected for inclusion in this special issue on culture and emotion outline a new approach to the relationship between culture and emotion which extends beyond the universalism-relativism debate. One issue that is attracting increased research attention is the role of emotion language in emotion research. Three papers included here address the issue of language. A second theme concerns the distinction between individualism and collectivism and related cultural dimensions such as honour, and its implication for the experience and expression of emotions. Three papers address the effects of this cultural dimension; one is on crying, another on well-being and positive feelings; and a third on anger-related emotions. Finally, a last theme that is considered in this special issue is the way in which emotions are expressed in inter-racial interactions.

Contents

A.S.R. Manstead, A.H. Fischer, Beyond the Universality-specificity Dichotomy. **G.R. Semin, C.A. Görts, S. Nandram, A. Semin-Goosens,** Cultural Perspectives on the Linguistic Representation of Emotion and Emotion Events. **S. Kitayama, K. Ishii,** Spontaneous Attention to Emotional Utterances in Two Languages. **J.R.J. Fontaine, Y.H. Poortinga, B. Setiadi, S.S. Markam,** Cognitive Structure of Emotion Terms in Indonesia and The Netherlands. **M.C. Becht, A.J.J.M. Vingerhoets,** Crying and Mood Change: A Cross-cultural Study. **N. Basabe, D. Paez, J. Valencia, J.L. Gonzalez, B. Rimé, E. Diener,** Cultural Dimensions, Socioeconomic Development, Climate, and Emotional Hedonic Level. **P.M. Rodriguez Mosquera, A.S.R. Manstead, A.H. Fischer,** The Role of Honor Concerns in Emotional Reactions to Offenses. **B. Mesquita, M. Karasawa,** Different Emotional Lives.

ISBN 1-84169-924-1 2002 200pp. £39.95 hbk
A Special Issue of *Cognition and Emotion*

www.psypress.co.uk

Forthcoming!

MOTIVATION AND EMOTION

Philip Gorman

(A-Level Teacher, Stafford College, UK, and Examiner and Team Leader for the AQA-A Level Examination Board)

"This is a very good text that covers the main topics in the area of Physiological Psychology very effectively, in a user-friendly tone. The numerous progress exercises throughout the text are well thought through and will encourage students to think carefully about the meaning, as well as the content of the text." **Kevin Silber, Staffordshire University**

Motivation and Emotion covers both the psychological and physiological explanations for these aspects of human behaviour. The brain mechanisms that govern motivations are discussed and questions such as 'Why don't we eat ourselves to death?' and 'How do we know we are thirsty?' are answered. Types of emotional responses and explanations of emotional behaviour are covered. The book analyses psychological, physiological, and combined approaches to theories of motivation and emotion.

Philip Gorman gives an accessible account of these important topics. Motivation and Emotion makes an ideal introduction to this areas of physiological psychology.

Motivation and Emotion is a concise, cheap, and accessible book designed for the modular AS/A2 syllabi. It is written by experienced an A-Level teacher and examiner and includes all textbook features common to the books in the Routledge Modular Series such as essay examples, progress and review exercises and a glossary.

Contents
Motivation and the Brain. 1: Hunger. Motivation and the Brain. 2: Thirst. The Biological Basis of Behaviour. Psychological Theories of Motivation. A Combined Approach to Motivation. Emotion and the Brain. Explaining Emotional Behaviour. Study Aids.

ISBN 0-415-22769-0 Summer 2002 160pp. £27.50 hbk
ISBN 0-415-22770-4 Summer 2002 160pp. £7.99 pbk
Routledge Modular Psychology Series

www.psypress.co.uk

SHAME AND GUILT

JUNE PRICE TANGNEY
(Department of Psychology, George Mason University, Fairfax, USA)
RONDA L. DEARING
(VA Maryland Health Care System, Perry Point Division, USA)

"Among the human emotions, shame and guilt have been relatively neglected by psychologists and other behavioral scientists. Moreover, work on these topics has been hampered by fuzzy conceptualization, armchair theorizing, and inadequate reliance on empirical research. In one fell swoop, Tangney and Dearing have remedied this situation... Shame and Guilt is an outstanding work of scholarship, as meticulously researched as it is interesting and readable. It will become an instant classic in the literature on emotion."
- **Mark R. Leary, PhD,** Wake Forest University

Shame and guilt have captured the attention of scholars and clinicians for generations, but have only recently begun to be subjected to systematic empirical scrutiny. This book reports on the growing body of knowledge on these key self-conscious emotions, integrating findings from the authors' original research program with other data emerging from clinical, social, personality, and developmental psychology. The authors demonstrate that shame and guilt have significant — and surprisingly disparate — implications for many aspects of human functioning, with particular relevance for interpersonal relationships. The book examines such compelling topics as the varying levels of empathy shown by "shame-prone" and "guilt-prone" individuals; links to anger, hostility, and aggression; and effects of shame and guilt on psychological adaptation and moral behavior. Clinical applications of the research are discussed in depth, as are methodological and assessment issues; developmental considerations; and implications for parenting, education, and social policy.

Contents: What is So Important about Shame and Guilt? What is the Difference between Shame and Guilt? Assessing Shame and Guilt. Our Intrapersonal Relationship: The Self in Shame and Guilt. Moral Emotions and Interpersonal Sensitivity: Empathy Enters the Picture. Shamed into Anger?: The Special Link between Shame and Interpersonal Hostility. Shame, Guilt, and Psychopathology. The Bottom Line: Moral Emotions and Moral Behavior. Shame and Guilt across the Lifespan: The Development of Moral Emotions. Sex, Romance, and Conflict: Shame and Guilt in Intimate Relationships. Implications for Therapists: Shame and Guilt on Both Sides of the Couch. Looking Ahead: Implications for Parents, Teachers, and Society. Appendices: A. *Tables.* B. *Measures.*

1-57230-715-3 2001 264pp. £26.95/$35.00 hbk
Emotions and Social Behavior Series
Published by Guilford Press

For orders originating in the UK and Europe please telephone +44 (0)1264 343071

For orders originating in the US and Canada contact the Guilford Press on 800-365-7006

Psychology Press
Free Email Alerting Service!

The free Psychology Press email alerting service enables you to receive email notification of new books and offers in your area/s of interest. Updates are sent approximately once a month and members can unsubscribe at any time. We respect the privacy of our customers: we will always include a link to leave the list in any communication and will never pass on your email address to a third party.

To join any of the lists, simply send a blank email to the relevant address from the list below:

Abnormal Psychology .... abnormal.psychology-join@psypress.co.uk

Biological Psychology .... biological.psychology-join@psypress.co.uk

Cognitive Psychology .... cognitive.psychology-join@psypress.co.uk

Comparative and Behavioural Psychology ....

comparative.behavioural.psychology-join@psypress.co.uk

Developmental Psychology .... developmental.psychology-join@psypress.co.uk

Educational Psychology .... educational.psychology-join@psypress.co.uk

Evolutionary Psychology .... evolutionary.psychology-join@psypress.co.uk

General and Introductory Psychology ... general.intropsych-join@psypress.co.uk

Memory .... memory-join@psypress.co.uk

Neuropsychology .... neuropsychology-join@psypress.co.uk

Philosophy of Psychology .... philosophy.of.psychology-join@psypress.co.uk

Research Methods and Statistics .... research.methods-join@psypress.co.uk

Social Psychology .... social.psychology@psypress.co.uk

Sport Psychology .... sport.psychology@psypress.co.uk

Work Psychology .... work.psychology@psypress.co.uk

To subscribe online, visit **www.psypress.co.uk** and select *Email Alerting*